BUSINESS ESPIONAGE
Risk, Threats, and Countermeasures

BRUCE WIMMER, CPP

ELSEVIER

AMSTERDAM • BOSTON • HEIDELBERG • LONDON
NEW YORK • OXFORD • PARIS • SAN DIEGO
SAN FRANCISCO • SINGAPORE • SYDNEY • TOKYO

Butterworth-Heinemann is an imprint of Elsevier

Butterworth Heinemann is an imprint of Elsevier
225 Wyman Street, Waltham, MA 02451, USA
The Boulevard, Langford Lane, Kidlington, Oxford OX5 1GB, UK

Copyright 2015 © Elsevier Inc. All rights reserved.

No part of this publication may be reproduced or transmitted in any form or by any means, electronic or mechanical, including photocopying, recording, or any information storage and retrieval system, without permission in writing from the publisher. Details on how to seek permission, further information about the Publisher's permissions policies and our arrangements with organizations such as the Copyright Clearance Center and the Copyright Licensing Agency, can be found at our website: www.elsevier.com/permissions.

This book and the individual contributions contained in it are protected under copyright by the Publisher (other than as may be noted herein).

Notices

Knowledge and best practice in this field are constantly changing. As new research and experience broaden our understanding, changes in research methods, professional practices, or medical treatment may become necessary.

Practitioners and researchers must always rely on their own experience and knowledge in evaluating and using any information, methods, compounds, or experiments described herein. In using such information or methods they should be mindful of their own safety and the safety of others, including parties for whom they have a professional responsibility.

To the fullest extent of the law, neither the Publisher nor the authors, contributors, or editors, assume any liability for any injury and/or damage to persons or property as a matter of products liability, negligence or otherwise, or from any use or operation of any methods, products, instructions, or ideas contained in the material herein.

Library of Congress Cataloging-in-Publication Data
A catalog record for this book is available from the Library of Congress

British Library Cataloguing in Publication Data
A catalogue record for this book is available from the British Library

For information on all Butterworth Heinemann publications
visit our website at http://store.elsevier.com/

This book has been manufactured using Print On Demand technology. Each copy is produced to order and is limited to black ink. The online version of this book will show color figures where appropriate.

ISBN: 978-0-12-420054-8

Working together
to grow libraries in
developing countries

www.elsevier.com • www.bookaid.org

Dedication

This book is dedicated:

To all those who have undertaken the challenge of protecting companies from business espionage and especially those who want to get even better at effectively dealing with the challenges of business espionage. This includes Robert Dodge of G-4S, Tatiana Scatena do Valle of Pinkerton Brazil, James Acevedo of Andrews International, the late Dan Grove of Hill & Associates, and Tim Johnson of Technical Security Consultants, Inc., all of whom gave me invaluable information and insights on global business spying.

To my colleagues working with Business Stratagem Support Group, G-4S, I-SeRVE, and Pinkerton (a Securitas Company) where I have had the opportunity to help businesses protect themselves from business espionage. It is worth noting that I have made some changes in dates and details, where it is not relevant to the ultimate matter, in order to protect the companies involved and the details they have shared.

To my wife, Teresa, my beloved helpmate and sweetheart who tolerated the time I dedicated to writing this book while working full-time.

To my daughter, Ashley Teeter, who assisted by using her graphic arts talents to illustrate some concepts in this book.

And, to the Lord, who sustains me!

CONTENTS

AUTHOR BIOGRAPHY

Bruce Wimmer, CPP, is the Director of Business Stratagem Support Group, a consulting company that specializes in countering business espionage and related security threats. Mr. Wimmer has more than 43 years of experience in countering business spying. He served in the United States Air Force for nearly 22 years, as an intelligence officer and mostly as a Special Agent with the Air Force Office of Special Investigations (AFOSI) where he specialized in counterespionage and worked closely with a number of U.S. and other government's counterespionage agencies around the world. During his time with the Department of Defense, he was cited for developing the best and most comprehensive counterespionage education and awareness program in the entire U.S. Air Force. A "red team," which posed as a hostile intelligence service to test security effectiveness, was surreptitiously sent to target and test the most critical resources in his area of responsibility—the entire team, including the team's supervisor, were detected and "apprehended" within two days when an educated and aware workforce detected the team and reported their suspicions to Mr. Wimmer's AFOSI detachment. He was also cited for having the largest actual espionage investigations caseload in the U.S. Air Force and was responsible for the neutralization of multiple internal and external Air Force spies. After retiring in 1994, he joined Pinkerton Asia and began working with businesses to protect their sensitive information in an international business environment and working with the oldest and largest private security firms in the world. Mr. Wimmer has authored numerous articles in journals and magazines, chapters in books, and is a regular speaker at professional security venues. He has appeared on CNN, CNBC, National Public Radio, ABC/Discovery Channel as well as television and radio from Taiwan to Pakistan, and Hong Kong to Colorado and Florida. He has been interviewed by such international publications as Newsweek, Business Week, the International Herald Tribune and USA Today.

INTRODUCTION

Espionage has, by its very nature, always been a mysterious and secretive activity. The very words "espionage" and "spying" conjure up all kinds of images in most people's minds. Since espionage usually involves covert and clandestine activities, many people's eyes glaze over when the subject is mentioned. As a result, when it comes to espionage or spying in the business sense, there is often a great deal of confusion and a very real lack of understanding.

Business espionage is often cited as being one of the oldest businesses in the world. It certainly goes back a long time and most historians will cite the loss of the silk secrets from China to Japan, Korea, India, and Europe as the oldest documented cases of business espionage. That means, at the very least, it goes back to around 300 B.C.

This book was written because, in the twenty-first century, business espionage is a major threat to businesses and economies around the world. It is vitally important for the business leaders to better understand it in order to devise countermeasures to protect their most sensitive business information. If businesses continue to think that business spying is the stuff of James Bond and that it does not threaten them, they will continue to suffer massive and even catastrophic consequences.

Before one can effectively address the topic of spying in the corporate/business world, it is important to understand the terminology. Currently there are at least five English-language terms used to describe the same general business threat. They include:

1. Business espionage
2. Corporate espionage
3. Industrial espionage
4. Commercial espionage
5. Economic espionage

All five of these terms refer to the same general subject area. Economic espionage is often used to differentiate between government/military national security espionage (which is what many people think of when thinking of the subject of espionage) and economic-related spying (which takes place in the business sector). However, because business technologies can have dual or military applications and because some governments own businesses or directly control businesses, it is not always possible to clearly differentiate government spying from business spying.

At least this term makes it very clear that the espionage has an economic aspect to it.

In fact, there are many who believe that the national security of any nation-state is so closely tied to its economic well-being that even the more exclusive business espionage has a national security aspect.

Generally speaking, however, the terms "industrial espionage," "economic espionage," or "corporate espionage" are all used when spying is conducted for commercial or business purposes and not purely national security purposes. Economic espionage is often used to refer to spying conducted or orchestrated by governments and it is usually international in scope. The terms industrial or corporate espionage are more often more intra-national and occur between companies or corporations who are competitors. Business espionage can include both sectors when the government is directly involved in the business sector, and, again, this happens in many places around the world. For example, in some countries there are state-owned enterprises that are a part of international business but a nation-state controls the business. Additionally, in an increasingly global economy, it is difficult to differentiate between international and intra-national.

For purposes of this book, all five terms will be used somewhat interchangeably to refer to the theft or misappropriation of sensitive proprietary information for businesses, especially intellectual property. The latter will usually be called "trade secrets."

The term trade secret refers to one of the four major categories of intellectual property:

1. Patent
2. Trademark
3. Copyright
4. Trade secrets

Trade secrets are the main focus of business espionage and can include a formula, pattern, compilation, program device, method, technology, technique, or process that has value and is not generally known—at least when it is stolen. Additionally, in most jurisdictions, in order to get legal protection there must also be a documented, provable effort expended to keep this information secret and known only by those who need to know the information to effectively do business. While patents, trademarks, and copyrights are also subject to theft and/or misappropriation, it is trade secrets that are most often the target of business spies. While there are important legal definitions and distinctions, this book will refer to trade secrets as sensitive business information even if the owner did not take appropriate steps to protect that valuable information, which means it may not legally be a trade secret. These are all important terms to understand as we explore the world of business espionage.

Business espionage misunderstood

As mentioned earlier, there are a number of misconceptions and misunderstandings that impact the lack of effective security for sensitive business information. Some of the most significant include what we will call the silo syndrome, the James Bond syndrome, an exclusive cyber-security focus, and the ostrich syndrome. Since they are so common, I think it is important to discuss some of the typical barriers faced in more detail.

Silo Syndrome

During a security conference (U.S. State Department's Overseas Advisory Council, or OSAC) in Washington DC in 2012 a panel of experts in counterespionage identified this syndrome as one of the biggest issues facing those who must deal with business espionage. Many companies look at business spying as a problem that needs to be assigned to some isolated organizational functional silo within the corporate structure. Common departments it gets pushed to include security, IT, legal or human resources, where business spying becomes their problem. "It's a security problem" or "it's an IT problem" are frequently heard. The conference's panel of experts agreed that business spying should be considered as a business problem, not just a security or IT problem. This means the business entity, as a whole, must deal with the problem and the approach must cut across multiple organizational functions or silos. That is, it must be embraced by a leader in the organization who has the power and ability to cut through these functional silos and bring the entire organization together to address the problem.

James Bond Syndrome

There are also widespread misconceptions that industrial/corporate/business espionage is only a high-tech crime perpetrated by James Bond types who are envisioned as rappelling into a business office or manufacturing site suspended from thin special wire cables in an air conditioning duct. Or, if that's not the case, at least it is viewed as a crime perpetrated by nerdy but genius computer hackers. Neither one could be further from the truth. As we will learn, just about all corporate spying is accomplished using decidedly simple, and preventable, methods.

Regretfully, because so many companies have a poor understanding of, and protection from, business espionage it means that a bumbling Maxwell Smart (Note: Maxwell Smart was a spoof character also known as Secret "Agent 86" on a television series called "Get Smart," which was a situational comedy spy show that was on television in the United States from 1965–1970) rather than a James Bond could easily steal valuable business secrets from all too many businesses.

Exclusive Cyber-Security Focus

The IT world has done such a good job addressing intellectual property loss issues that some experts have erroneously concluded that cyber-security is the focus of countering business espionage. While information on a computer can be extremely valuable and definitely warrants protection in any counterespionage approach, the same piece of information written on a scrap of paper can be worth just as much. Especially since business spies often gather bits of the puzzle and begin to assemble it into viable and useable intelligence. It is therefore important to protect all forms of sensitive business information regardless of how it is stored. The sensitive information can be in a cyber-based form, but it can also be paper/document based, photographic, observed, or oral/spoken. It can be formal documents, draft documents, working papers, or scrap, and it can be internal correspondence or communication, even financial, legal, or regulatory. It can also be conversations that are part of formal meetings, informal meetings, or casual conversations. While there is definitely a cyber-security component and IT security has to be involved in any twenty-first century counterespionage program, focusing on computer-based data protection alone can leave an organization extremely vulnerable to other basic business-spying techniques.

The core target of business espionage is "information." In the world of business espionage, sensitive information is best defined as any knowledge that can hurt your organization and/or help your competition. Again, that information can be in any form.

According to the U.S. Federal Bureau of Investigation (FBI) and similar international law enforcement organizations, industrial espionage costs U.S. companies alone anywhere from $24 billion to $250 billion annually.[1] Experts concur that the technical (usually cyber) vulnerabilities are responsible for less than 20% of all losses or compromises of sensitive business information but most agree that the cyber-threats seem to be growing. Again,

---

[1] FBI Press Release, July 17, 2002.

cyber-security is critically important but a business should definitely not put all of its counterespionage efforts into the IT realm alone because that leaves up to 80% of threat vectors unaddressed.

Most business spies are perfectly happy to get information from the easiest and most overlooked and, hence, least protected of sources—including trash, a vulnerable telephone, or an employee that talks too much and too freely. As a matter of fact, those sources are even preferable, because they often involve less risk to the spying operative. A good spy always looks for the path of least resistance and the least likely to be detected. Those methods will be tried first before trying anything fancy or high tech. These methods can also make it easier to exploit IT security. It might mean social engineering or observation to get a password, but it might also include planting a spy inside the company or recruiting a spy who has some legitimate access to IT systems. Or it might involve exploiting physical security vulnerabilities to get direct access to a server or communications line.

Ostrich Syndrome

Sadly, many business executives (and this includes information managers and security officers) do not believe their organization will be targeted, a belief based primarily on "hope" rather than factual analysis. It is very similar to the ostrich sticking its head in the sand when a threat emerges. Assuming that if their company is not in the defense industry or is not highly technical... or if it is relatively small, no one will try and steal its business secrets. In fact, one of the most frequently expressed misconceptions is, "Our business has nothing worth stealing or our technology is changing so fast that by the time it is stolen, it will be obsolete." This all-too-common attitude gives business spies their best opportunities. In fact, small businesses tend to be targets more often than large corporations, simply because there are more of them (and more competitors) and they tend to have far less security. No company or organization is immune to being targeted by business spies. To a small company, a $50,000 loss could be much more devastating than the loss of billions would be for a large company. If you truly have nothing worth stealing (hence worth protecting), you probably should not be in business because you are not really competitive. When conducting a security risk assessment, this attitude frequently surfaces, but after talking in business terms about what the company does, how they do it better than their competition and what their objectives are for the next 1–5 years, it soon becomes clear that they do have trade secrets, even if they have not identified them as such. It also often means they may be missing key legal qualifications for their trade secrets and do not have measures in place to protect their sensitive information.

Another aspect of the ostrich syndrome has to do with a desire to quickly implement changes and programs. For example, when a company decides to move some of their manufacturing to another country, they want it done quickly and they do not want to see or hear any "evil"—that is, anything that might slow the process down. As a result, many companies make catastrophically bad decisions that are made without even considering business espionage and loss of intellectual property as a part of the overall decision-making process.

Objective

The main objective of this book is to make it clear to businesses of all types and sizes, all around the world, that business espionage is very real and is a threat that can significantly impact a business. Business spying is pervasive and it can do grave damage to businesses. But it is probably more important, armed with that kind of knowledge, to understand that it also possible to protect yourself and your business from the threat of business espionage.

How to Use This Book

This book is organized into two major parts:
1. The problems posed by business espionage
2. The countermeasures that can protect a business entity from spying

The first part provides insight on why business espionage is an important business issue. It examines the threats, typical vulnerabilities, and the business consequences (or, when these components—threat, vulnerabilities, and consequence/business impact—are combined is considered the "risk") through a series of case studies and other background information. The second part covers cyber and physical countermeasures. But most importantly it stresses the importance of having integrated countermeasures for the most effective risk-based protection possible.

The purpose of all of this is to provide an understanding of the threat that can be used for pro-active planning or education/awareness. It includes identifying any gaps or vulnerabilities in effective security for business spying so a business can close these gaps and reduce its vulnerability to the threats. Looking at these two components (threat and vulnerability), along with business impact issues, this book will provide guidelines for reducing your risk to business espionage threat.

UNDERSTANDING THE PROBLEM OF BUSINESS ESPIONAGE

1

UNDERSTANDING THE RISKS

Abstract

This chapter explains the terms 'risk' and 'risk assessment.' It explains how the terms sometimes get misused and the meaning of the terms in this book. Risk is a combination of the likelihood of occurrence of threats, the gaps in effectiveness from standards or vulnerabilities, and the consequences or business impact. The goal of this book is to base countermeasures and programs on risk-based solutions.

Introduction

It is important to understand that the best-structured approach to determining how to enhance protection from business espionage is to have countermeasures that are risk-based. In order to do that, it is important to regularly do a thorough and complete risk assessment. That risk assessment becomes the basis for your company's counter espionage program.

Having said that, it is important that you do a true and complete risk assessment, not a partial one that someone might, in error, call a "risk assessment." It sounds simple but I find people often and mistakenly interchange or misuse terms. This is especially true of the terms threat and risk, or people will use the term "risk" in some other context. In the context of this book, we will be using the term risk to mean a very specific security issue. As we have already noted, this approach to risk draws on a number of international programs and standards and we will be applying these standards to risk as it relates to business espionage.

For example, I have had a number of security directors or business leaders say to me something along the lines of: "The People's Republic of China is a high-risk environment for business espionage and sensitive business information." As we will learn in Chapter 3 (and we will see more examples in other chapters where there are case studies), the People's Republic of China has been involved in, or in some way linked to, a number of business espionage situations. Therefore, it may be valid to say the People's Republic of China is a "high threat" environment, but before we can say it is "high risk" we have to look at how effective your existing security measures are and the consequence levels for your business processes/information there. These two factors are also part of risk determination. Risk is not based entirely on threat, although threat is a factor in determining a security risk.

During discussions about their various operations within the state of Nebraska, in the United States, another security director assured me their operations in Nebraska were "low risk." When I asked why, that security director said: "Everything in Nebraska is relatively low risk. Everybody knows everybody in Nebraska and it is pretty isolated from a lot of these traditional outside security issues." My response was, "Maybe it is low risk in Nebraska and maybe it is not, but first we must thoroughly examine the threats in Nebraska, USA." Then, I shared with him that we needed to see how effective their existing security was in Nebraska and, finally, how critically important the processes/information were for the company when it came to its Nebraska-based operations. Only then could we say what the true security risk was for the company's Nebraska-based sites.

Therefore, if you have been mindful of the criticality levels for information that will be available in and to China and have implemented good, strong security measures (hence your vulnerability is low), you may find the threat is high but the vulnerability and consequence are low enough to make the risk acceptable in China.

For example, in Nebraska, the threat might be low but security efforts there might be plagued by complacency ("nothing ever happens here" attitudes) and thus are not very effective (high vulnerability), which could also be where some of the most critically important information in the company resides (high consequence/business impact). This means the threat is low but vulnerability and consequence are high.

In fact, in this hypothetical situation, the company's business espionage security risk in Nebraska is higher than in the People's

Republic of China. Maybe the threat in China is higher than in Nebraska but the overall risk (adding the vulnerability and consequence factors) is higher in Nebraska. Unfortunately, I frequently see this kind of dichotomy in discussions about countering business espionage.

This is why it is so important to understand the differences in terminology and to be precise and consistent. Threat levels and risk levels between the two locations could be very different.

So, before you decide on a pro-active counterespionage program and what countermeasures your business should have in effect, you must have a thorough understanding of the threats, the vulnerabilities, and the consequences/business impact. Together they make up business espionage security risk. Armed with that knowledge you can determine the countermeasures that should be employed to mitigate business espionage risk at any given entity. This is risk management at its best, and this is the approach we will be working from as we examine business espionage security risks.

Risk Methodology

For purpose of this book, business espionage security risk will be defined using a methodology adopted by the International Standards Organization (ISO), the U.S., British, and French governments, Sandia Laboratories, among many security organizations, and others. It is basically the potential for an adverse outcome assessed as a combined function of threats, vulnerabilities, and consequences associated with incidents, events, etc. This combination, as we hinted above, results in business espionage security risk. The same process can work for all kinds of security-related risks such as executive protection, terrorism, theft, workplace violence as well as business espionage. This can allow a candid comparison of risks that truly compares "apples to apples." To compare and prioritize, it is important that we use the same methodology for all business-espionage-related risks.

Risk Formula

As a result of approaching business espionage in a risk-based manner, companies and individuals have a means for determining how they can best focus their limited time, effort, and money on lowering their vulnerabilities and protecting their most important information from the most likely threats. The risk equation is often depicted as:

$$\text{Risk} = \text{Threat/Hazards} \times \text{Vulnerabilities} \times \text{Consequences}$$
$$\text{Likelihood of Occurrence Gaps from Standards}$$
$$\text{Business Impact/Value}$$

When risk management is applied to the process, the formula changes slightly to incorporate countermeasures, which can lower the vulnerabilities or lessen the direct consequences. That formula then looks like this:

$$\text{Risk} = \frac{\text{Threat/Hazards} \times \text{Vulnerabilities} \times \text{Consequences}}{\text{Countermeasures}}$$

In an environment where there are significant issues with business espionage we need to analyze threats using a threat assessment approach. This threat assessment should focus on who is targeting businesses (especially similar businesses), what businesses they are spying on (does location, size, etc. matter?), and how they are spying on businesses (determine their most likely *modus operandi—or methods of operation*). You can get this type of information from a variety of sources. I highly recommend joining professional security associations, such as ASIS International, and using the membership to create relationships with similar companies. If you share some information, they will likely do the same. Depending on your nationality, you can liaison with the national agencies responsible for countering espionage in your country. You can also talk with the security attaché or equivalent position in the embassy when you have business entities in a foreign country. There are other professional associations such as chambers of commerce, etc., in various countries. Once again, by building relationships you can share and ask about the issues and situations in a given country or business sector. By talking with all of these different entities you can begin to formulate a threat picture of the espionage situation in a given location. Your focus, again, should be on the methods used by business spies within your given location of concern and the likelihood of occurrence for business spying.

The next step is looking at the security standards that should be in place to protect the business from the business-spying threat as determined in the threat assessment. We will then identify any gaps that currently exist in how the company is operating versus these established/accepted standards for the overall threat they face. This is determined in the vulnerability assessment phase of the risk assessment. These gaps will be identified and labeled as "vulnerabilities."

A good approach to determining the effectiveness (lack of effectiveness is the definition of a vulnerability) of your existing security and identifying vulnerabilities is to focus on how well your security measures fulfill four major security functions. Ask yourself, how well does existing security. . .

- Deter,
- Detect,
- Delay, and
- Respond.

Deterrence is a difficult measure to determine and quantify, but it is important to know the threats and put yourself in the mindset of the threat vectors. For example, if I were going to try and get inside of this facility posing as a legitimate employee or someone authorized to be inside the facilities, how easily could I do this? How thorough is the access control? Can I piggyback? How should I be dressed? Who provides service here and how quickly are they given access or checked? Can I dress and pose as a delivery person, repair or maintenance person?

When there is signage and barriers, and when it is apparent that employees and security are extremely alert, the result is deterrence. A potential spy decides the opportunity for success is low and the opportunity of being detected is high. From the bad guy standpoint: time to try another place or another method. Deterrence has value.

It is also important to determine how effective your means of *detection* are. Typical means of detection include alarm notifications or computer penetration attempt alerts. It also includes being spotted on CCTV, or being spotted by a security officer or an alert employee. Detection includes the awareness of a possible problem but it also includes reporting it. An employee who says, "Yes, I saw that and it was suspicious to me. I wondered about it," but does nothing and does not notify security, police, or some response element then it is not true detection. The "alertness" was only part of the process. Having a CCTV system that is not monitored but simply records does not count as true means of detection. It may help in a follow-up investigation, after-the-fact, but it is not a means of early detection. For CCTV to be a part of a detection process, it almost always has to be monitored by trained and dedicated staff or security personnel. It cannot be a part-time job. It needs to be a dedicated function.

The key to any detection is a quick, timely response that interrupts or prevents the perpetrator from completing the attack on your sensitive information. Once there is detection, and notification, there is usually a time gap before a responder can get to a site. If someone is able to break into the computer server area, for example, but a motion detector sets off an alarm in the security control that indicates someone is inside the server room, it will take a period of time (hopefully only a few minutes) for a responder to get there. The key is to have sufficient delay mechanisms in place that will allow enough time for the responder to arrive. This is the *delay* mechanism. Ask yourself, what is the earliest likely detection of unauthorized access? If it is an alarm on the outer door to the Research and Development area, then you must assume that the unauthorized individual entering is already inside by the time the alarm signal is received. There is usually some time spent trying to verify the authenticity of the alarm and once that is done, a security officer (for example) will need to be dispatched. This is the final part of the response. If this process takes 5 minutes and it takes another 5 minutes for the officer to get to the server room, 10 minutes has expired since first detection. If absolutely nothing can be done in 10 minutes, then you are okay. But if someone can grab a media and get back out, you did not have sufficient delay built-into your security approach. Perhaps there needs to be a locked metal storage cabinet with sufficient strength and locks that can resist at least 10 minutes of "attack" where sensitive media are stored. Maybe a secondary room with a solid door and lock is what is needed. This is what effective delay is all about.

Now we have already addressed the response to some degree but detection without response is largely worthless. When the first vehicle alarms became popular it became common to walk out into a parking lot and hear two or three car alarms going off. No one paid any attention and no one was responding. The audible alarm was designed as a "detection" system but without a "response" it was worthless. If you have a computer system that detects a possible penetration attempt, it is important to see what the response is. How long does it take for the response? And, of course, the question then is: how effective is the response? For example, if you have an unarmed security officer responding to a break-in and the intruder is armed with an AK-47, you had a response but the response was not appropriate. The key is to get both a timely and an effective response for the situation that was detected.

This is a structure for conducting a vulnerability assessment. You must have all four components, and they must interact to have effective security and not have vulnerabilities.

Depending on the likelihood of occurrence/threat issues and the consequence/business impact analysis (the third part of the risk assessment), we can determine which of the identified vulnerabilities warrants being lowered by implementing various countermeasures. This can even help determine the priority of implementation of countermeasures. A good strategy would be to first implement the countermeasures that can most significantly lower the risk. If you cannot implement all countermeasures, focus first on those that give you the biggest "bang for your buck" or for the time you have invested.

For example, if your threat assessment determines that your business has a relatively high potential threat for business espionage and that the *modus operandi* of most of the current business spies in the industry and location/locations of concern have been to try and piggyback (follow employees with legitimate access) into the production area to view processes being used there, you might want to focus on your access control standards for the production area.

If, during your vulnerability assessment phase of the risk assessment, you see that there is a considerable amount of piggybacking going on because there is no turnstile and people are entering/exiting and even holding the door open for others, you have to decide if the threat warrants a security officer being stationed there to better control access, or if a turnstile needs to be installed. Maybe that solution, combined with improved employee security (education and awareness) training, could sufficiently lower the vulnerability because employees might begin to understand why they cannot hold the door open for others to enter.

If you cannot protect the entire production area, you might also try and determine if are there any areas where there are some special and sensitive methods or processes being used. Can those be further segregated and access to those areas enhanced, as opposed to trying to invest in strengthening access control for the entire production area? These are consequence-related issues. Or maybe the controls do need to be high for the entire area because the most sensitive information is throughout the area. Once these questions are answered in your consequence/impact assessment, you can determine which of the access control measures needs to be implemented and you will know exactly why (threat and consequence based) you did what you did.

Another strategy is to implement simple and low-cost countermeasures quickly. This "low hanging fruit" may not have as big an impact on lowering the overall vulnerability as another countermeasure but implementing several of these can become an important vulnerability- (and hence risk-) lowering countermeasure. Senior management like these because the cost is low and yet there is a reduction in vulnerability/risk. Examples of "low hanging fruit" might be changing some processes (requiring a government identification when signing in on a roster), a trained and effective escort for visitors, and general or specialized security training.

In this book we address various aspects of business espionage threat. We will focus on the types of businesses being targeted (the diversity of which is apparent from the case studies in Chapters 3, 4, 5, 6, 7, and 8) and on looking for who might be behind the business-spying efforts and, finally, on what methods they are likely to use (also summarized in the case studies). That kind of thorough threat assessment is the first step in an accurate, up-to-date risk assessment. But understand that it is nearly impossible for a business to lower the threat. The threat is largely impacted by outside entities that can include nation states. While a company likely cannot neutralize a threat on its own, it can understand the threat and plan countermeasures that blunt the threat with strong security measures. Strong security measures can sometimes even deter a potential threat.

You should also look at the typical vulnerabilities and gaps in the current security program and how to evaluate those. That vulnerability assessment will suggest the most important corrective actions and/or new/enhanced countermeasures. The ability to reduce vulnerabilities is an important part of lowering risk for a business.

When considering vulnerabilities it is also important to have good security procedures, policies, and standards. The standards must be realistic and effective against the threats faced. If you do not have a good understanding of the standards that should be employed, go with the basic security standards established by various professional security associations (e.g., ASIS International). Many of the basic physical and IT security standards will apply to most threats.

We will focus on the types of businesses being targeted (the diversity of which is apparent from the case studies in Chapters 3, 4, 5, 6, 7, and 8) and on looking for who might be behind the business-spying efforts and, finally, on what methods they are likely to use (also summarized in the case studies).

Summary

In summary, it is important to remember that the vulnerabilities identified probably lead to the most important corrective actions/countermeasures and implementing these can then, in turn, lower business espionage risk. Again, there is little that can be done by a company to lower threats. For example, weather events such as tornadoes or hurricanes are out of our control, and even state-sponsored espionage is bigger than most companies can neutralize on their own. Furthermore, you cannot give your competitors integrity; they either have integrity built into their company culture or they do not.

Companies can sometimes reorganize processes or diversify supply chains, for more redundancy and less exposure than what a consequence assessment has identified. This can lower the consequence score and reduce risk, but even that is sometimes difficult to achieve. So, the main way you can lower your risk is to lower the vulnerability score and that means reducing the number of security vulnerabilities you have, which makes your business a "harder target" for those who would try and spy on you.

In this book, business espionage security risk drives the need for countermeasures. It helps companies determine how much of their limited resources they should allocate to counter business espionage.

By properly focusing your security efforts and optimizing, not necessarily just maximizing, your efforts you can effectively deal with business espionage threat and greatly improve your overall protection against business espionage. The fundamental building block for all of this is a good, solid risk assessment that includes a threat assessment, a vulnerability assessment, and a consequence/business impact assessment. These are then combined to create a more complete risk picture, which is the underlying approach of this book when examining business espionage.

Whether some business leaders recognize it or not, intellectual property is the lifeblood of an enterprise. It is important to protect that "lifeblood," and we will be addressing how to do that throughout the book but especially through the countermeasures detailed in Chapters 8, 9, 10, and 11.

2

CHARACTERISTICS OF BUSINESS SPIES

Abstract

This chapter includes information on how you might "profile" a business spy. It examines the motivation of spies through the acronyms MICE and CRIME. While the truth is that there is no "typical" spy, there are some personal traits that frequently emerge and these can be used as possible "red flags" for more closely examining the background of someone who might be given access to sensitive business information.

One of the 64,000-dollar questions that may be asked over and over again is: How can we identify a spy in our midst? Are there any common traits? Is there something we can look for? Is there a "profile" of a typical business spy?

I have been involved with a number of studies that have tried to answer that question and I think it would be worthwhile to go over the results that came from some of the most detailed and comprehensive among them.

MICE

I have found that one of the most accurate ways to look at the motivation of a spy is often summarized in the acronym: MICE. The MICE acronym is used by almost all government counterespionage agencies around the world. The acronym MICE stands for Money, Ideology, Compromise, and Ego.

Having dealt with many spies over my 40+ years in the counterespionage business, this simple acronym sums up the majority of the motivations I've seen. It does not matter if the spy was working for a government or was totally in the business environment; there are usually at least two or three of these motivations present. In an ongoing, mature espionage situation, all four may be present. Most of the time the initial motivation will be ideological and/or money. When talking about "ideology" we are not talking just about a political ideology. This also includes the company culture, power and promotions, etc. That may be how it starts but the ideological motivation quickly includes money, as the "customer" starts rewarding the spy for results. When a spy, who was doing this for ideological/psychological purposes, starts getting rewarded with money and goods, this quickly becomes yet another motivator. Good spy handlers will identify weaknesses that can be coercively used if necessary (for example, threats of compromise) in an emergency. But most want to try and stroke the spy's ego because that can be much more effective in motivating a results-producing spy. Positive motivations usually beat negative motivations. Once again, the spy's ego can develop into a powerful motivation. Many spies for governments have been assigned high military or civilian ranks and even had covert meetings in uniforms of the nation they were spying on. All of this is designed to drive home how valuable the individual is to the "mother country." This ego and pride quickly emerges as another important motivator.

Of course, money is a chief motivator and even when the motivation initially was ideology and ego, when money is added, it becomes yet another powerful motivating factor.

A good example of this is highlighted in a U.S. Federal Bureau of Investigations video entitled "Game of Pawns" that was developed to prepare (education/awareness) students who were going to the People's Republic of China. It was based on the real-world story of Glenn Duffie Shriver who, in 2010, pleaded guilty to conspiring to provide national defense information to the People's Republic of China and was sentenced to 4 years in federal prison.

The story of how he got there forms the heart of the movie—and the FBI's warning: "We'd like American students traveling overseas to view this video before leaving the U.S. so they're able to recognize when they're being targeted and/or recruited." The docudrama opens with some stock Oriental wisdom: "There is an old Chinese proverb: Life is like a game of chess, changing with each move," intones the narrator. "And to win the game you must often sacrifice your pawns." Enter Shriver. We see the American, then 24 years old, greeting Chinese friends on campus ("What up, dog?") and partying with Chinese women. "It was going to be the best year of my life," he says. "Shanghai was amazing. It fit me like a glove." Shriver's zest for China got a little out of hand. Short on cash and unsure of what to do with his life, he answers an online ad looking for essays on U.S.-China relations. A woman named Amanda, who would become his handler, pays him $120 for his thoughts on international affairs and praises his handi-work. After a few meetings, she takes him to meet her colleague, Mr. Tang, who keeps the flattery coming. "What impressed me most about your paper, Glenn, was your insight into the Chinese mind," he tells him. "Most Westerners make no attempt to truly understand us." It is hard to know what the real Shriver was like at the time, but China expatriates will certainly see something familiar in him. Like many young people who come to study or work in China, this Shriver seems bright, curious, and well-meaning. He also seems rather full of himself—willing to believe, for instance, that he, more than others, truly understands China. Willing to believe that his insight, in the form of short essays, could be of genuine interest to powerful people may be incredibly naïve, but Shriver was only 24 years old, and they were paying him. Skilled handlers were also stroking his ego. Thus, we have a combination of ego and money motivations. As his relationship with Amanda and Tang develops Shriver twice takes, but flunks, a U.S. State Department test. The Chinese give him stacks of U.S. cash nonetheless. Things escalate when they suggest he apply to work at the CIA. In the movie, Shriver hesitates: "What, um—what exactly are you asking me?" In the next shot, as he gazes out at the Shanghai skyline, he calls them back and makes his play: "I'm going to need $40,000 to start." The rest of the FBI video tracks his inevitable downfall, complete with a dramatic scene at U.S. customs, a failed lie-detector test, and an on-plane arrest as he tries to flee. Some things are obviously not covered in the video but we do know Shriver is doing 4 years in federal prison for accepting a total of $70,000 in return for information. The film was posted on the FBI site along with a prison-cell interview con-ducted with Shriver where he talks about how he was wooed by his handlers, and admits to being driven by greed. "You know when you're having money thrown at you especially when you're at a place like Shanghai," he says. He then falls back on the film's "pawn" metaphor: "You know we live in a very sheltered society," he says. "And when you go out among the wolves, the wolves are out there."[1]

In addition to my own experience, I have talked extensively with individuals involved in counterespionage from the U.S. Central Intelligence Agency (CIA) to the U.S. Federal Bureau of Investigations (FBI), British MI 5 to the former Soviet Union's KGB officers. Several things always came out of those conversations. Spies tend to be nervous people. They know they are betraying someone's trust and probably violating laws so the challenge is to convince them that they will not be caught. What concerns a spy, then, are things like changes in their level of affluence or a polygraph examination that can mean they are under investigation or will be soon. Government-controlled spies have been given elaborate escape plans to demonstrate how much their host spy agency cares about the safety of the spy and their security. The question the spies wrestle with is how they could possibly explain why they have more money than they should have or why they copied a certain document that is clearly out of their working sphere. If they are traveling a lot to foreign destinations (where the laws might not be so stringent or the government is compliscent in the espionage) could someone ask them about this travel? What they want is help concocting a story that could deflect suspicion. Interestingly enough, many spies, even in the business world, ultimately have said they wanted to get out of that business after a while. Yes, it is exciting and they got a lot of money, but it is very stressful and difficult to rationalize over the long term. The spies admit that, at some point, their conscience begins to bother them. The one thing that spies will often say is that there was a point in time when they would like to have stopped but they did not know how to get out of the spy business once they had been doing it for a while.

CRIME

Another acronym that addresses the motives of business spying, and is used by a number of government counterespionage organizations is "CRIME." In this case the five spying motives are Compromise, Revenge, Ideology, Money, and Ego.

---

[1] Emily Rauhala, "FBI Movie Warns U.S. Students Not to Spy for Chinese," *Time Magazine*, April 16, 2014.

This model shares four elements (Compromise, Ideology, Money, and Ego) with the MICE model. What I like about this model is that it addresses another element that I sadly see all too often: the revenge aspect.

In some ways this might be covered by ego and ideology, but there is a specific revenge motivation that sometimes surfaces. Perceived mistreatment by co-workers, management, or "the company" in general can result in an individual deciding to contact competitors and make those who mistreated him/her pay for their misdeeds. Once again, that might be the first and primary motivation but many other motivational factors are often quickly added to the *raison d'être* for the spy.

BECCA

The Business Espionage Controls and Countermeasures Association (BECCA) has analyzed a number of espionage cases and come up with some conclusions and identified some trends. For example BECCA says the breakdown by sex (male or female) is about 50-50. Half are male, half are female—so there is no trend there.[2]

BECCA did note that the majority of spies were college graduates but with what they termed a "low-value degree." The majority of spies have also had a broad employment history but one with a number of short-term positions (job hopping). This means the majority of spies moved around a lot and do not have any deep commitments to a company. Most have money problems. Often they get lower pay than some of their counterparts and, as a result, have self-esteem problems. Personality-wise, most spies are "loners" and do not have many close friends within the company. Because they typically are not constrained by rules, if you review their driver's license record there will be a number of issues or tickets. Interestingly, a lot of spies said they had originally wanted to go into law enforcement or the military as careers but some physical disabilities, etc., precluded it. Even though we are talking espionage, not workplace violence, a number of spies have extensive interest in firearms. Finally, BECCA found that many spies reported they had exciting or romantic hobbies.[3]

[2]Business Espionage Controls and Countermeasures Association notes, http://www.becca-online.org/images/Forensic_Incident_Responce.pdf
[3]Ibid.

Project Slammer

In the United States Department of Defense, there was a study I was familiar with that has now been partially disclosed and publicized. It was known as "Project Slammer" and it was designed so that military clinical psychologists and other experts could do in-depth interviews with convicted spies to see how they looked at themselves and what they had done. Several interesting and potentially worthwhile factors emerged. Most spies looked at themselves as "special" and "unique." In other words, they had strong egos. Here is that "ego" motivation again. They believed that the spying they did was no different than what a lot of other people did. Maybe others were not spies but they were also doing unethical or illegal things to get ahead. Specifically, most believed that spying was a "victimless crime." They, in fact, believed they were not "bad" people but blamed the company and its poor security for why they became spies. If poor security wouldn't have allowed spying to take place, they would not have become spies, they reasoned. Furthermore, according to them, the poor security processes put in place in regards to spying proved the company did not really care. Also they said they believed that if they were truly "being taken care of" by the company, they never would have become spies. According to them, the company mistreated them, did not recognize their talents, or somehow had done them wrong. So, once again, it was someone else's fault that they turned to spying. Finally, they also admitted they liked the excitement of the spy business but some did acknowledge they might have stopped if they could have avoided paying a big penalty for their actions.

U.S. FBI

Finally, the U.S. Federal Bureau of Investigations has put together some indicators of potential spying that also apply to the internal spy. The FBI found that many spies work odd hours for no apparent reason. Spies also regularly take information home or copy it. Additionally, spies are particularly unhappy with policies and procedures about software and downloading, or other controls. The majority of spies were also known to take short trips to foreign countries for unexplained reasons. They might have one trip that had some possible rationale but then would often go back a month or two later for no apparent reason. Anyone who previously engaged in personal contact with competitors, especially international competitors, could be suspect. This is especially true if they had undue affluence and appeared to buy things such as residences, cars, etc., that they should not have been able to afford. The majority of spies admitted that they had a many career disappointments and had been overwhelmed by life crises when they decided to resort to business spying. Finally, the FBI found that the majority of spies felt guilty and became almost "paranoid" about people watching their activities at work so they would plant cameras to video their workspaces and would "trap" drawers or doors to try and determine if someone opened them and if they were being watched or investigated.[4]

Other factors the FBI cited as possible indicators that someone might be involved in spying include:

1. Greed or Financial Need: A belief that money can fix anything. Excessive debt or overwhelming expenses.
2. Anger/Revenge: Disgruntlement to the point of wanting to retaliate against the organization.
3. Problems at Work: A lack of recognition, disagreements with co-workers or managers, dissatisfaction with the job, a pending layoff, etc.
4. Ideology/Identification: A desire to help the "underdog" or a particular cause.
5. Divided Loyalty: Allegiance to another person or company, or to a country besides the home country of the business.
6. Adventure/Thrill: Want to add excitement to their life, intrigued by the clandestine activity, "James Bond Wannabe."
7. Vulnerability to blackmail due to things such as extra-marital affairs, gambling, or fraud.
8. Ego/Self-image: An "above the rules" attitude, or desire to repair wounds to their self-esteem. Vulnerability to flattery or the promise of a better job, often coupled with Anger/Revenge or Adventure/Thrill.
9. Ingratiation: A desire to please or win the approval of someone who could benefit from insider information with the expectation of returned favors.
10. Compulsive and Destructive Behavior: Drug or alcohol abuse, or other addictive behaviors.
11. Family Problems: Marital conflicts or separation from loved ones.[5]

---

[4] "An introduction to detecting and deterring an insider spy," the Federal Bureau of Investigations, http://www.fbi.gov/about-us/investigate/counterintelligence/the-insider-threat
[5] Ibid.

Summary

An analysis of these various studies certainly establishes that there is no absolutely clear profile of a spy. No one or two things that always shout out: "Spy!" However, there are some things that you can watch for and be alert for. Supervisors, people working in sensitive areas, human resources staff, etc., should especially be aware of these potential indicators and they should be considered in screening for hiring, promotions, or for periodic re-screening.

Human resources and managers should keep in mind that someone who is not satisfied with their job or who has had a lot of broad but short-term jobs warrants a little more attention. This could be a sign of someone who feels underappreciated and recruiters of spies really like this kind of person. Keep this in mind if these characteristics seem prevalent and the individual in question will have access to especially sensitive, high-business-impact information.

Supervisors should be especially alert when individuals do not want to take any vacation time and work a lot of additional hours or claim no one can do their job. If that is not normal for the job position, it warrants a closer look.

Some other characteristics that could be a "red flag" include those personnel that always seem to ignore established policies and procedures, especially those relating to information and document security. Even if the individual is not a spy, per se, they may be indirectly supporting business espionage by leaving sensitive information lying around or throwing sensitive pieces of the information puzzle into the trash where spies can "mine" it.

Employees with access to sensitive information that are known to have serious money problems and issues should be watched more closely. For example, if they have issues with traffic tickets and/or their driver's licenses, even if their job does not directly involve having a valid driver's license, these problems can be a potential indicator that warrants further monitoring.

From a countermeasures standpoint, what we can learn is that the better security a company has in place and the more seriously it takes business spying, the less likelihood that an employee will resort to becoming a spy. In fact, if there are countermeasures in place and someone is checking work hours, undue affluence, and foreign travel some business spies said they would not have resorted to spying because it would have been too risky. If someone is monitoring compliance with counterespionage policies and procedures and, if there is even the possibility of a polygraph, many spies say they would not have gotten involved. They would have been deterred.

Figure 2.1 What if a nice, innocent looking gentleman (left) shows up at your company and expresses an interest in using your company to produce a new item and the potential for sales volume looks extremely lucrative. So lucrative, in fact, that your sales staff are going to show him some sensitive research and development labs and production processes on a tour that showcases why he should use your company for this new business. You remind him that no photographs are authorized and proceed on the tour. Maybe you even ask him to leave his mobile device and briefcase in the meeting room. The photograph on the right details some of the other ways this innocent looking gentleman might be taking unauthorized pictures and recording information. Your caution with the briefcase and mobile device could be well placed but your action has only eliminated two out of at least six possible camera/recording devices. Maybe more. What about his glasses, the microphone/camera in his tie, the pen he is carrying in his chest pocket and his watch? All of these audio/video recording devices can be purchased on line or on the internet. You realize, too late, that this supposedly nice, innocent looking gentleman was a spy for your competition and now they have some of your trade secrets and they just won a competitive bid.

Employees and supervisors should be educated on business espionage and encouraged to make reports directly to their supervisors or, as a minimum, via an anonymous hotline if they suspect some unusual work habits, contact with competitors, undue affluence, or trips to foreign locations that are not directed by the company as a part of work. Employees that participate in professional conferences, especially in high-threat environments, should be monitored and reminded that they are not authorized to discuss sensitive information. Supervisors and employees should be educated on these "indicators" and the need to report their concerns.

If someone is already involved in espionage against your company, you would probably want to encourage these individuals to stop such activity. Therefore, consider dealing with their rationalization for spying by offering to help anyone who inadvertently got caught up in the spy business an opportunity to "get out." This is very similar to employee-assistance programs when someone has a substance-abuse problem. This might get to someone who has decided he or she wants out of the spy business. It can give them a way out and is worth considering, as long as the company legal representatives are involved in the process.

Finally, it is apparent that individuals who have ties to other companies or other countries (look especially at the top dozen countries where business espionage is widespread in Chapter 3) are more likely to be business spies statistically. While this certainly should not be a sole factor for hiring or granting access to sensitive information, it is something that should not be totally ignored either.

Remember, too, that there are outsiders who can also be business spies. The copy machine/printer repair staff, the delivery person, the new potential client at your booth during an industry convention or the potential new customer who comes to talk about new business. Your facilities staff, your company leadership and your sales and marketing staff also have to be aware of the potential threats and should be trained to be careful in volunteering sensitive information from a good social engineering elicitor. The business spy is probably not going to fit your stereotype of a spy because there is no stereotype. Anyone could be a business spy.

So, while there is no simple formula or clear profile of a business spy, there are some "red flags" and indicators that warrant further attention by those responsible for protecting a company's business secrets. Knowing these indicators and making them part of a comprehensive counterespionage program is important. It is another tool in the counterespionage arsenal.

3

HIGH-THREAT LOCATIONS FOR BUSINESS ESPIONAGE

Abstract

This chapter includes information on which geographic regions and countries have a high threat when it comes to business espionage and examples of why. The threat is high in Asia – especially in Greater China (including the People's Republic of China, Hong Kong SAR and Taiwan) Korea, Japan, the Philippines, Singapore and India. There is also a high threat in Latin America, especially Cuba, Venezuela, Brazil and Mexico. The high threat locations in Europe include Russia, France and Germany. The Middle East includes the Israelis and most Arab countries. Even in Africa, especially South African and Zimbabwe, there are substantial business spying threats.

Certain geographic areas and countries are known for being a source of high levels of business espionage activity. It is important

Business Espionage
© 2015 Elsevier Inc. All rights reserved.

for businesses to know business spying threat is higher when company personnel are traveling there or when a company is planning on doing business there. In this chapter we will examine some of the highest threat regions and countries. It is important to differentiate between locations where the spying occurs and the originating source of the espionage activity. The focus here is on the originating source.

Asia-Pacific

The Asia-Pacific region may have some of the most robust business-spying activities in the world. One of the most common high-threat locations to be examined in this chapter is what we will term "Greater China." This includes the People's Republic of China, Hong Kong SAR, and Taiwan. All of these locations have experienced a large number of business-espionage-related incidents, where the *modus operandi* employed is complex and often involves inter-related attacks.

Other Asia-Pacific "hot spots" for business espionage include Japan, the Republic of Korea, Vietnam, India, and Singapore.

Latin America

Elsewhere in the world, but often overlooked when it comes to business spying, is Latin America. Latin America is another high-threat environment for business espionage. The Cuban intelligence service, the DGI (Directorate General for Intelligence), is very active in Latin America and is known to run a number of business espionage operations and will even resell the information to raise money. The Venezuelan intelligence services are also known to be involved in business espionage, as a result of learning a lot from the Cuban DGI. While the government intelligence agencies may not be as directly involved as Cuba and Venezuela, business espionage is also widespread in Mexico, Brazil, and other Latin American countries.

Europe

Europe is another area where there can be a high level of business espionage activities. Countries that particularly fit into this category in Europe include Russia, France, Germany, and even Switzerland. The latter country is listed because it was home to one of the earliest business intelligence schools (Geneva School of Business Administration) and has one of the largest concentrations of "competitive intelligence" activities in the world, mainly centered in Geneva. At least a dozen companies that specialize in competitive intelligence have their headquarters in Switzerland. One of these firms (Alp Services) allegedly targeted the French nuclear firm, Areva, for sensitive business information and the food giant, Nestle, was convicted of having a private security officer infiltrate an anti-globalization activist group (ATTAC) in order to learn what was going to be in a study and book the group was preparing.[1] As we have noted, there is sometimes a fine line between competitive intelligence and business spying.

While there have been several complaints about the Germans being involved in business spying in the automotive and aerospace world, it is interesting that Germany claims that one of the biggest business-spying threats emanates from France. The head of the German satellite company OHP said France steals more intellectual-property-related technology from Germany than does China or Russia.[2] Public reports indicate that the Service 7 element of the Directorate General for External Security (DGSE) actively targets business interests, and in recent years the French have allegedly planted moles in U.S. companies such as IBM, Texas Instruments, and Corning in order to steal their business secrets and provide that stolen sensitive business information to the French Compaignie des Machines Bull.[3]

Germany is certainly not innocent; in fact, it is home to a number of business-spying incidents. Germany's intelligence service is called the Bundesnachrichtendienst or BND. Since the 1960s the Germans have been actively involved in spying on the U.S., France, Great Britain,and Italy. The BND reportedly regularly monitors telecommunications of foreign corporations with operations in Germany. The BND is also active within the U.S. Reportedly German agents have cultivated moles (planted spies) in a number of U.S. firms according to colleagues in U.S. counterintelligence agencies. Within the counterintelligence world, the BND is gathering extensive information in the fields of economy, technology, and industry.

[1] "Nestle Guilty of NGO Espionage," EuroNews, January 31, 2013, http://www. euronews. com/2013/01/31/nestle-guilty-of-ngo-espionage-
[2] "OHB-System to Build German Optical Spy Satellite," Aftenpost, November 11, 2009 http://www.aftenposten.no/spesial/wikileaksdokumenter/article3985652.ece#. U4uV6ijwo6o
[3] Peter Schweizer, "The Growth of Economic Espionage: America is Target Number One," Foreign Affairs Magazine, January/February 1996.

The leak of National Security Agency (NSA) documents by insider spy Edward Snowden prompted international outrage. However, while uninformed citizens may have been genuinely surprised and upset, government intelligence agencies around the world were not surprised. For example, Bernard Squarcini, the head of the French Direction Centrale du Renseignement Interieur (DCRI)—France's counterintelligence agency—noted of the controversy: "The Americans spy on French commercial and industrial interests and we do the same to them."[4]

Interestingly enough, there were a number of recent reports that the BND had arrested some spies within their ranks who were supposedly providing sensitive information to the U.S. In fact, as a result of those arrests, the supposed station chief of the U.S. Central Intelligence Agency in Berlin was recalled after an incident.[5] This is consistent with the fact that the U.S. Central Intelligence Agency's former Director, R. James Woolsey, Jr. declared no more "Mr. Nice Guy" and promised that U.S. intelligence agencies would be looking for unfair trade practices and industrial espionage directed against American firms.[6]

Still, it would be difficult to find a country in Europe that is more involved in business spying than Russia. Russia is, of course, led by a number of former Committee for State Security (KGB) agents. For them, espionage was a way of life and when they took over many of the government and quasi-government business entities, business spying was naturally followed.

After some reorganization, the FSK (Federal Counterintelligence Service), the counterintelligence core of the former KGB and FSK, became known as the Federal Security Bureau (FSB). The foreign intelligence portion of the FSK became the Foreign Intelligence Service (SVR).

When Vladimir Putin came to power, he instituted a plan to make the FSB something like his old KGB. He has worked to reconsolidate most of the splinter intelligence agencies back under the FSB, correcting much of the inefficiency that existed among the separate agencies and making the new combined agency stronger and more effective. Putin has also worked to ensure that the FSB receives extensive funding to train, recruit, and modernize the intelligence services. Currently, the SVR remains separate from

---

[4] "Paris Also Snoops on U.S.", Agence France-Presse, October 26, 2013, http://www. arnewsupdates.blogspot.com/2013/10/. . .also-spies-on.html
[5] Greg Miller and Stephanie Kirchner, "Germany Orders CIA Station Chief to Leave Over Spying Allegations," *Washington Post*, July 10, 2014.
[6] Peter Schweizer, Friendly Spies: How American's Allies Are Using Economic Espionage to Steal Our Secrets, published by Atlantic Monthly Press, 1993, pp. 186-187.

the FSB, but other crucial components such as the Federal Border Service and Federal Guard Service have been reintegrated, as has the Federal Agency of Government Communications and Information (FAPSI), Russia's equivalent of the U.S. National Security Agency.

Additionally, Putin has tapped many former KGB and current FSB members to fill positions within Russian big business, the Duma, and other political posts. Putin's initial reasoning was that those within the intelligence community thought of Russia the same way he did—as a great nation, both domestically and internationally. Putin also knew that those within the intelligence community would not flinch at his means of consolidating Russia politically, economically, and socially. It could be argued that Russia has become an "intelligence state" under Putin.

Since the fall of the Soviet Union in 1991-1992, foreign corporations have been very busy in Russia as they scramble for market share and seek to meet growing demand for consumer products. For these companies, growing Russian nationalism and tension with the West increases both the chance of regulatory and legal hassles and the possibility that Russian intelligence activity might be directed their way. In other words, as tensions rise, so could the threat, and hence risk, for Western and Asian corporations.

Not all these problems are new. As a KGB officer, Putin became an intelligence star by successfully stealing technology from the West. He has since encouraged Russian intelligence agencies to expand their collection programs with the awareness that such business-related information can boost the Russian economy. The Russians have become very pragmatic. They do not see the need to spend the money to develop a technology from scratch when they can steal or buy it for a fraction of the cost and effort.

In the wake of the 9/11 attacks, counterintelligence agencies in the United States and many other Western nations focused on counterterrorism missions and diverted counterintelligence resources for that purpose. It would take several years for the domestic counterintelligence efforts to get back to their pre-9/11 levels. Russian intelligence services, like the Chinese, have taken advantage of that window of opportunity to recruit sources and obtain critical information from foreign companies. Additionally, the Russians have gone to great lengths to steal intellectual property from foreign firms operating inside Russia, either by infiltrating their companies with planted agents or by recruiting employees. Currently, if you are operating or visiting in Russia, you can expect to have the intelligence agencies such as the SVR and FSB trying to get business secrets. I have had a dozen or more instances where companies have had incidents in hotels or offices within Russia that made it clear someone was monitoring calls and computer communications and individuals had been going through documents and computers left in hotel rooms.

Two classic examples have emerged recently. During the Winter Olympic Games in Sochi, Russia, the Russian Deputy Prime Minister Dmitry Kozak let it slip that some of the bathrooms in Sochi hotels have cameras monitoring activities. This should be no surprise as the hotel rooms, including bathrooms, are regularly monitored in a number of countries. . .China and Russia just being two of them. Likewise, the Russians also released detailed telephone transcripts of conversations between Victor Yanukovych, president of Ukraine, and Victoria Nuland, U.S. Assistant Secretary of State for European Affairs, where Nuland allegedly used an expletive in reference to the European Union. What is incredible is that two government officials would talk on mobile telephones so openly and not know or, perhaps care, that the conversation could be monitored.[7]

Africa

South Africa and Zimbabwe have expressed an interest in benefitting from business spying. Some African leaders have noted that many Asian economies were supposedly kickstarted by counterfeiting and stealing trade secrets.[8] The Robert Gabriel Mugabe School of Intelligence, in Zimbabwe, started in 2007 and began graduating its first students in 2010. The school has included the African Union Committee on Intelligence and Security Services. Interestingly, the school was heavily funded by the People's Republic of China. Among the areas the school supposedly focuses on is what the school calls "economic" matters.[9]

Middle East

Finally, there are the Israelis, who are renowned for their business spying. However, it is important to remember that nearly all the intelligence agencies of most Middle Eastern nations will

[7]Austin Petersen, "Russian Spy Cameras In Bathrooms Report No Problems," The Libertarian Republic, February 6, 2014. http://www.nydailynews.com/sports/olympics/sochi-olympics. . .

[8]"Ultimate Guide to Intellectual Property Protection," *CSO Magazine*, June 6, 2012.

[9]"Mugabe Launches Robert Mugabe Intelligence Academy," Reuters, October 26, 2007, http://www.reuters.com/article/2007/10/26/us-zimbabwe-mugabe.

collect business-related information during the course of their intelligence activities. Some experts from within the intelligence communities have rated the Israeli intelligence services capabilities as among the top four of the world (along with the U.S., Russia, China). Israeli spying in the business arena tends to be more in military areas. The case of Michael Haephrati and his wife is an exception to that as in this case an independent Israeli computer programmer created a Trojan program that allowed his customers (Israeli private investigators) to potentially spy on their client's competition— for a price.

Counter Punch published an article on March 12, 2009, by Christopher Ketcham, detailing the Israeli methods of operation. "Israel conducts an aggressive and damaging espionage campaign in the U.S. this sensitive issue is never mentioned in the media or discussed by the government, mainly because of the special, sensitive relations between Israel and the U.S. and the influence of the Israeli lobby, which punishes any American lawmaker that dares to criticize Israel." According to Ketcham, proof can be found in the annual "Business Espionage" FBI report to Congress. Israel is reported as a hostile intelligence threat second only to China—and by a small margin. In the 2005 report, for example, the FBI claims that "Israel conducts an information gathering campaign in the U.S." [10] A 1996 report by the Counterintelligence Services, a branch of the Pentagon, contained a warning that "Israel considers scientific data gathering in the U.S. to be its third priority, right after information gathered in the neighboring Arab states and information on American policy decisions regarding Israel."[11] According to a U.S. CIA report the infiltrations used by Israeli intelligence are perpetrated using advanced methods.[12]

Former FBI Deputy Director for counterintelligence, Harry B. Brandon, reported in a congressional hearing that "Israel is looking for business information as well as military secrets. One of the best methods they have is exploiting business partnerships between Israeli and American firms which supply software to the entire U.S. market and the various government agencies. In this way they get access to the information they're looking for."[13]

---

[10] National Counterintelligence Executive (ONCIX), Annual Report to Congress on Foreign Economic Collection and Industrial Espionage, 2005.

[11] Christopher Ketcham, "Israeli Spying in the United States," Counterpunch, March 12, 2009. http://www.counterpunch.org/2009/03/12/israeli-spying-in-the-united-states/

[12] IBID

[13] Jaque Martin, "Israeli Spying in the United States," The European Union Times, March 21, 2009. http://www.eutimes.net/2009/03/israeli-spying-in-the-united-states.

The primary Israeli business espionage collection agency is called the "LAKAM," and is one of Israel's most effective intelligence organizations. LAKAM is a Hebrew acronym for the Israeli Defense Minister's Scientific Liaison Bureau. Its agents operate in the United States, Japan, France, Germany, Italy, Great Britain, Switzerland, and Sweden. LAKAM's biggest operation is inside the U.S. Their agents operate out of the Israeli embassy in Washington. D.C. and have two other offices—one in Los Angeles and the other in New York City. Their operations in these cities are believed to include 35 full-time agents with several dozen more informants. Israeli industries/companies that benefit the most include aerospace, chemical producers, and electronics firms.

In addition to regular agents, Israel also uses deep-cover agents posing as business people and scientists traveling to the United States or other countries. Most of the time the agents are in direct contact with the Prime Minister's office and will use diplomatic pouches to transport the most sensitive information or materials.[14]

More Examples

The following are some specific examples that illustrate why some countries/regions are considered as "hot spots."

Business Espionage in/from Greater China

Over a period of years, going back to the late 1990s and into the twenty-first century, a large international manufacturing company with operations in China came under persistent espionage attack within the People's Republic of China by what they believed to be state-sponsored intelligence entities and by competition that was obviously being supported by the government. It was difficult to determine whether the competitors were directly involved in the spying efforts but the government was clearly involved based on the scope and scale of the monitoring going on.

One of the most significant recent public cases involved a May 19, 2014 indictment of five Chinese military officers the U.S. government alleged were from the People's Liberation Army Unit 61398. According to the indictment, five officers were involved in multiple cyber-spying efforts against five metals

[14] http://www.thefreelibrary.com/Allies+. . .+or+enemies.

and solar energy/green companies and a labor union in the United States.[15] One of the examples cited was a classic cyber-spying phishing incident where the alleged Chinese hacker created a fake email account claiming to be Nissan CEO Carlos Ghosn, then an Alcoa board member. The hacker sent a file called "agenda.zip" to approximately 19 Alcoa employees supposedly presenting an agenda for an upcoming shareholders' meeting. At least one of the recipients downloaded the file, which was a computer virus that allowed the hackers to gain access to Alcoa's network where they stole some 2907 emails and 863 attachments.[16]

It is also worth noting that there have been dozens of reports of attempts to recruit foreign students in China. The most notable is detailed in Chapter 2 where Glenn Duffie Shriver, an American student in Shanghai, was recruited and paid US$70,000 to go back and join a government agency and send information to China. There are nearly 15,000 American students studying in China. Meanwhile, the Chinese reportedly send nearly a quarter of a million students to the United States, for example, and counterintelligence sources suggest that at least half of these students are given instructions to gather information of interest for intelligence agencies. News media reported that Australian counterintelligence officials said that Chinese intelligence officials were building spy networks in Australian universities—where some 90,000 mainland Chinese students study.[17]

The Chinese countered that there have been efforts by foreign spy agencies to recruit Chinese students abroad and even within China. Clearly the use of students warrants counterespionage concern.[18]

The espionage acts I am personally aware of came from multiple threat vectors, including some of the following examples.

First, all of the offices of a large multinational manufacturing company's China headquarters in Beijing were subject to electronic and physical monitoring. Several discreet physical searches were carried out and several electronic transmitters were discovered. These were in devices implanted into office equipment, in electrical outlets, and even in dropped ceilings. Systems used in

---

[15] Devlin Barrett and Siobhan Gorman, "Chinese Charged in U.S. Hacks," *Wall Street Journal*, May 20, 2014.
[16] Danny Yadron, "Breach of Alcoa Emails Relied on Simple Phishing Scam," *Wall Street Journal*, May 20, 2014.
[17] Julie Makinenr and Tommy Yang, "China, U.S. Go Tit for Tat Over Student Spying Cases," *Los Angeles Times*, May 7, 2014.
[18] Ibid.

their internal office conference room were able to be intercepted as they broadcast throughout the building and immediate area.

Expatriate employees complained about things being moved and "rifled" within their offices and files in their offices specifically moved. As a result, several covert traps were set and it became evident that documents and files were, in fact, being gone through and photographed by building "security" staff, "maintenance" staff, and "cleaning" staff that regularly went through office areas and files after work hours. A covert camera caught some of the searches. When locks were changed to the exterior doors, building security demanded access. Their "excuse" was that there might be a fire, electrical problem, or plumbing issue. Once the company gave them a key, then immediately changed the lock and the next day building security came to demand a "key that works." When asked if there was a fire or problem the previous evening, there was simply a look of disdain and an insistence that a working key be provided.

Out of the more than 300 employees working in the corporate headquarters in China, approximately 20 were identified, over time, as formal sources planted, recruited, and working for the government. This identification took place over the period of several years by talking with other employees who were aware of whom the government sources were. However, while these were the main government monitors, all employees were subject to being asked to cooperate with the government or face consequences.

All telephones within the offices appeared to have been monitored and recorded. At the time there was a maximum capacity for recording and when the recording capacity was reached, the phones would automatically inactivate and there was no dial tone for a period of up to 10 or 15 minutes while changes were made to apparently allow more monitoring.

Once an employee had sensitive documents disappear from her office. She said she was concerned that the documents could have fallen from her desk into her trash. The security manager (an expatriate known as the "asset control" manager) went down to the basement of the high rise to talk with the janitorial services staff. He was not expected and as he walked from the garage to the trash room on the same level, he found hundreds of documents pulled out of the trash, separated and laid out on the floor. When some of the cleaning staff noticed him standing at the door they told him that the reason they were pulling the documents out was because there was a separate paper recycling service that paid them to do that. But it was clear the documents were also being looked at for content.

One of the cleaning staff worked during days in the office area and seemed to frequently be cleaning in an area whenever sensitive discussions were taking place. When asked about the cleaning staff being present, the staff advised she was Chinese and did not speak English. However, upon observation, several things were said in English that would evoke a reaction and the cleaner did react. After being confronted, the cleaner admitted that she did understand English, even if she maintained she did not speak it well. The local and expatriate staff was shocked to find out a cleaning crew member could comprehend English that well. Looking back, they were certain that some sensitive discussions had been held in her presence.

All senior personnel and expatriates for this company had their own vehicle and driver. Each driver was apparently co-opted by government sources and required to give reports on the habits of each person they drove for. This was confirmed by several of the drivers. Additionally, it is possible they did covert recording but this was not confirmed. What was confirmed was the fact that competitors and suppliers clearly had inside information garnered during conversations or cellular telephone calls that took place while company officials traveled inside their company cars. Some specific information that was designed as a test surfaced later and that information was specifically provided during conversations and cellular telephone calls within the company vehicle.

All expatriates working for the company lived in just a couple of housing areas. Mid-level employees were given quarters in high-rise Western-styled apartment buildings and more senior executives had larger single-family dwellings as homes. However, all rooms had audio and video coverage wherever staff lived and regardless of their job and function. A number of expatriates noted that their bathroom mirrors would fog up when they showered except for one circular area on the mirror where it was determined a camera was located. There were hundreds of stories about how this monitoring took place. In the tower apartment complex, which was almost exclusively occupied by expatriates for many companies working in China, one floor was devoted to the monitoring equipment and staff. The elevators did not stop on that floor and the fire-escape stairwell doors were locked on that floor. A couple of staff did happen to see inside when they were using the stairs and someone opened a door. They reported a large amount of people and electronic equipment was being utilized on the floor.

One individual reported that her daily telephone calls from her apartment to the United States corporate headquarters offices could go no longer than 30 minutes without being disconnected. She said that no call could be placed for approximately 5 to 10 minutes after the call was inexplicitly disconnected but then the phones would "magically" function again.

Another individual went back to Europe on a three-week holiday. When he and his family returned, they were "greeted" with a huge telephone bill. According to the employee, when he confronted the management of the housing area they told him they would "look into it." After two weeks he went back and asked about the telephone bill. He astoundingly reported that they told him: "We had the tapes listened to during that period and you are right. It was not you and you are not responsible for those charges."

One employee had a "battle" with a locally manufactured washing machine one night. The machine had a unique safety feature to prevent injury from the spinning drum. The machine's release lever would lock for 30 seconds after the spin cycle ended. On one occasion, when the expatriate employee said he saw the machine had stopped, he tried to open it. He was in a hurry and accidently broke the lever off. After this, the individual said he simply walked through his apartment complaining about the broken washing machine and within minutes (mind you he never called building maintenance) a maintenance worker was at the door ready to fix the broken washing machine…from just walking around the apartment and complaining to the ceiling and walls.

Another time an employee reported that he and his wife were sitting at their dining room table holding a conversation during dinner. The wife began to complain about what she thought was "rude" behavior by Chinese staff in the changing room of the complex's swimming pool. The next day when the wife went to the pool she was shocked to hear the local staff running around saying: "Get away from her; that's the woman who complained about us." According to the family, the only discussion about the Chinese staff took place at their dinner table between the husband and wife the previous night.

In yet another incident, a wife was out in the elevator/stair lobby of the apartment complex on the ninth floor. There were some repairs going on in the lobby area and there was a hole in the floor. After she had been out for some time, security officers came up the stairwell and said to her: "Oh good you are okay. We had not seen you for a while and we were worried you might have had an accident out here where the construction is on-going. We are happy you are okay." The wife was surprised they would know she was not inside their apartment. While some of these examples include personal monitoring, the potential for gathering business information is obvious, which is the main reason for expending resources on monitoring business people and their families.

Another employee, who had some security expertise, noted that a surveillance team regularly followed him and was able to observe that his driver would coordinate with them each morning when he picked up the employee at his residence. One time, in a restaurant he frequented, one of the employees covertly asked him if he knew he was being followed by "Chinese police." He brushed off the surveillance by noting it was a government team assigned to "protect him," but he noted the surveillance was frequent.

Company visitors to China stayed in several Western-chain hotels. All of these hotel rooms were known to have audio-, and often video-, monitoring capability. Each room was also regularly visited by intelligence services. In one case, the rooms of senior executives were entered and business-related documents were examined. Computers were also turned on and copied. The question then became: okay—this happens to senior executives, but what about our routine, mid-level employee who travels? A covert camera and microphone were concealed in the room of a mid-level traveling employee and the camera uncovered a team entering the room and systematically searching it. At one point the government team found the camera and one of the search team asked his supervisor what to do since it looked like a "spy camera." The supervisor said to put it back and get out of the room because another Chinese intelligence agency had apparently already targeted this visitor.

In another instance, a large international company held a board of directors meeting at a major hotel in the Hong Kong SAR of China. The company had a reasonably good security approach for the meeting site that included access control 24/7 as well as a technical surveillance countermeasures sweep before and one ongoing during the meeting. There were also multiple cross-cut shredders available in the meeting area and all cell phones and computers were turned off and batteries removed during the meeting. However, it was impossible to control the conversations of board members outside of the meeting room. At one point, executives took a break and went to the restroom. Since they were heavily into the meeting agenda they were talking business as they exited and went into the restroom. Security representatives tried to caution them but they were ignored. Then one of the security staff went into the restroom adjacent to the meeting area and there was a known intelligence broker standing in the restroom, wearing a white uniform and handing out hot towels. Unfortunately, he could also overhear conversations carelessly carried on. When the security detail spotted the man, the security team chief immediately went to the hotel security and asked why this known intelligence operative was working in a restroom near their board of directors meeting. Hotel security and management said there was no attendant assigned to that restroom and they accompanied the security team leader. The group returned to the restroom only to find the individual had fled and was no longer there.

Business Espionage in Singapore

Early in the twenty-first century, a U.S. headquartered company decided to move its Asia-Pacific headquarters to Singapore because it was perceived to be more secure from business spying than within China, where the bulk of operations were taking place. While the threat is probably higher within China, there is still business-spying threat in Singapore. The company let their guard down and ethnic Chinese employees in their Singapore office were ultimately found to be providing information to Chinese competitors. The employees maintained, when confronted, that they had been pressured by their "bretheren" in China to help the Chinese people. A similar activity occurred in another company I helped in Singapore when targeted by an Indian competitor. The Indian competitor used ethnic loyalty to convince the Singapore employees of Indian ethnicity to provide information.

As this last example illustrates, business espionage does not fit into neat packages. Business spies from Russia and China, for example, may operate in multiple countries (Singapore and Taiwan). One example I was personally involved with involved a "retired" KGB agent. He attempted to join the ASIS International chapter in Taiwan, which I founded and was the head of at the time. He sought me out and pointed out that both of us had a kindred spirit and background...we were both retired intelligence/counterintelligence types who were now in the private sector, as he put it. He suggested that we could work together. When I explained the ethical approach I took to business spying, he suddenly disappeared from my social contact list but I saw him many times in Taipei meeting with various business executives and Taiwan government officials. Some of these were well known for being aggressive when it came to business spying.

I was also hired by a Taiwan aerospace company to determine if one of its staff was supplying information to Chinese competitors.

I took the approach that I was representing a large U.S. aerospace company, which I said did not want its name released. I went to the company and started meeting with the suspect's colleagues. I used the pretext of potentially recruiting the individual. I asked his colleagues, one-by-one, what this individual's strengths were. I also asked what his weaknesses were. I used an old trick where you share information learned from previous interviews to imply you know more in order to get more information. The truth of the matter was that each of the aerospace engineers I was interviewing was also interested in a high-paying job with this fictitious U.S. firm. As I introduced myself, I explained that I was looking for an individual that not only had aerospace engineering experience and expertise, but also someone with high integrity. As the colleagues gave me a superficial endorsement of the "candidate" that was the subject of my investigation, I would query them about his weaknesses. Bit by bit, several colleagues made references to this individual's frequent trips to the People's Republic of China. Finally, his roommate was interviewed and he stated that all of this guy's colleagues knew that he was receiving some money from the People's Republic of China for information. We pursued this in enough detail to establish that there was truth in the rumor. The investigation confirmed how easy it is to elicit information from workers and how frequent non-business travel to high-threat countries can mean there is a problem. It also shows that even within greater China there is military, political, and business spying taking place amongst entities like the People's Republic of China and Taiwan—both business espionage centers who spy on many businesses from around the world but that also spy on each other.

Business Espionage in Vietnam

In 2011, a team of U.S. executives traveled to Ho Chi Minh City in Vietnam to train and work with a team in a newly opened branch of the company in Vietnam. While the Vietnam branch was part of a global company they did not necessarily have all of the intellectual property available at the corporate headquarters. At one point during the training, the leadership staff of the Vietnam branch took the U.S. corporate visitors on a long lunch. Since one of the laptops being used was hooked up to a projector, the branch staff assured the visitors that they could leave the laptop behind and it would be secure. After returning from the lunch, the computer seemed to have some running issues. When the corporate visitors returned to the U.S. computer forensic specialists ran a test and discovered that all documents on the hard drive had been copied by someone in the Vietnamese branch office. Interestingly enough, the head of the Vietnamese branch office was a former senior official in the Vietnamese government and jokingly made the comment that you "never retire" from your responsibilities to your government.

Korea, Japan, and India

Other chapters (including chapters 4, 5, 6, and 7) have examples of business espionage in Korea, Japan, and India. We can certainly say, based on my experience in the Asia-Pacific region, that Korean and Japanese businesses aggressively collect and use business intelligence. Korean and Japanese businesses understand the value of information gathered using business espionage tactics, and they are not deterred from getting involved in business spying if it gives them a competitive advantage. As one Korean businessman told me, "You are crazy and don't care about your business if you are not out there collecting information from your competitors." In the following chapters examples of Korean firms involved in business spying will be given. In fact, one expert advised that for its size, South Korea is the most active business-spying country in the world.

Japan is bigger in terms of population and Gross Domestic Product (economically) so the business spying may not meet the per capita test when measured with Korea but rest assured that Japanese businesses are also very active in spying. While Japanese government intelligence agencies are not necessarily formally involved, at least two quasi-government agencies are well known for gathering business intelligence up to even encouraging and conducting business espionage. These include the Ministry of International Trade and Industry (MITI) and Japanese External Trade Organization (JETRO).[19] It was also well known when I lived in Tokyo that the Japanese government gave some training to Japanese businesses at a business spy-training center, known in English as the Institute for Industrial Protection. The spy school was located in Shinjuku, Toyko-to.

India is another country where there is a great deal of business espionage occurring. Often business spying in India is conducted by "private investigators" hired by companies. I have talked to more than a dozen good-sized private investigations firms in India and every one of them told me they field calls almost daily asking them to conduct business-spying operations against competitors.

[19] http://digilander.libero.it/business.mentoring/gathering_business_intelligence.html

Business Espionage in Latin America

Over a period of years, going back to 2010, a large international food manufacturer with operations in Latin America came under persistent espionage attack in Brazil and Mexico from what they believed to be competitors and/or by professional intelligence gathers on behalf of competitors.

The business espionage attacks came in various forms, including some of the following examples.

A U.S. government counterintelligence agency was explaining how important business spying is to a number of fellow intelligence agency personnel. To illustrate how government counterintelligence agencies tend to focus on government/military secrets this particular agent related how the debriefing of a defector from the Cuban DGI (Cuban intelligence service) went. The government counterintelligence officer asked the defector who his targets were. The defecting Cuban intelligence officer said, "We primarily targeted generals." Expecting the names of military personnel, the counterintelligence officer asked which generals. "Oh...General Motors, General Electric and General Mills" replied the former DGI officer. The story illustrates that even in countries that are somewhat isolated from the overall global economy, businesses are focused on obtaining valuable and exploitable business-related information.

Another Latin American example involves a food manufacturer holding a major sales conference in Sao Paulo, Brazil. Event planners came into Sao Paulo in advance and got a five-star hotel setup to host the business conference. They did hire a security company to provide some access controls and support, but the company did not ask for a risk assessment or security-related recommendations. The venue their advance team selected (without security being represented), included a large conference room with a glass wall and door that looked out onto a beautiful garden area the hotel maintained. The security team set up operations to provide access control into the main conference room, but there was no Technical Surveillance Countermeasures (TSCM) sweep to detect electronic penetrations or monitoring prior to the meeting and no TSCM monitoring during the meeting. When the security team saw there would be sensitive information on PowerPoint slides and a large screen, they advised the company's event management that sensitive PowerPoint slides should not be displayed without putting up some curtains or barriers for the window that was open to the outside. The company event management team and even senior company leaders balked, noting that the garden was a wonderful, beautiful setting and backdrop. During the meetings, the security detail continued to observe the outside area as best it could.

At one particularly sensitive point in the conference, an individual was observed in the outside garden. He had a camera and began taking pictures of slides through the window. When the security team deployed to try and catch him, the observer ran away.

In another instance, some sensitive strategic planning meetings were taking place in Brazil as a food manufacturer tried to come up with a specific strategy and budget for purchasing a local company. As they went through negotiations and made an offer, it was apparent that the local company knew the maximum the bidding company was prepared to offer and they exploited their knowledge to get the maximum available offer. The company being sold knew when the bid was too low and where to stop. A subsequent investigation determined that one of the administrative assistants who was attending the internal preparatory meetings and providing some support had suddenly resigned after the meetings. An outside investigation determined the individual had suddenly moved back to his hometown, which just happened to be where the local company's headquarters was located, within Brazil. A discreet check of the individual's financial records also determined that the ex-administrator had received a very large payment from the local company being purchased—it was nearly 2000 times his monthly salary. That was received after the purchase deal was completed and just before he resigned. The source of the "leaks" became apparent, and it is estimated that it cost the food manufacturer nearly $40 million.

In Mexico, the food manufacturer had a security officer who was discharged after stealing multiple portable hard drives from the company's office in Mexico City. The officer worked on the midnight shift and regularly volunteered to do patrols on his own. He took the master keys and regularly entered all the various offices, even locked offices. He also went through the cubicles in office areas. During his shift, several personal and company items disappeared. A review of CCTV coverage disclosed he had clearly taken some employee's personal items. But he was observed going into the office where one of the hard drives was located the night it went missing. One of the missing portable hard drives contained information on formulas and recipes for products. Another missing hard drive contained pricing information and included most of the company's customers. Once again, the fact that the only hard drives stolen contained sensitive information was an early indication that this could have been something more than just petty theft. Employees and management did not initially think about business espionage being a possible motive for the thefts, but after investigators pointed out the unlikely odds of this happening by accident, the company became more concerned and launched a full-scale investigation.

Another incident in Mexico involved a large international manufacturer of equipment and parts. This manufacturer operated a fairly sophisticated production facility. While much of the equipment was off-the-shelf equipment, the way the equipment was configured and how it was used was a sensitive trade secret. The company took what they felt were reasonable precautions to protect their methodologies. One day, an engineer walking around the workshop did a double-take because the janitor looked just like an individual with whom he went to the university. He called out the man's name: "Jorge, is that you? Hola!" The individual reacted but then tried to run away. Caught by security, the "janitor" admitted that he was really an engineer and advised he worked for a competitor. He told the security staff that he had been compelled by his employer to get hired as a janitor and spy. He regularly went back to the competitor company offices and advised them on what he observed, given the "free reign" he had within the facility. Mexican staff that worked at the manufacturing company was surprised that an engineer would "stoop" to working, even for a short time, as a janitor just to steal information. They were unaware of the business espionage threat and the value of the information to a competitor.

United States

While the majority of the business spying around the world seems to come from locations such as greater China, Japan, Korea, Russia, India, Israel, etc., there is also a great deal of business spying taking place within the United States. While, in my experience, a number of the business espionage cases within the United States involved foreign entities, the United States has also had a number of business-spying incidents within the country itself. Besides the matters covered in other chapters, there was, for example, the accusation that Hilton executives stole more than 100,000 sensitive documents from Starwood Hotels and Resorts.[20] In another matter, Proctor and Gamble staffers were accused, in 2001, of rummaging through rival Unilever's garbage for competitive information.[21] Certainly the United States remains a major target country and no company—large or small—within the United States should be ignoring the business espionage threat.

[20] Peter Lattman, "Hilton and Starwood Settle Dispute," *New York Times*, December 22, 2010, http://dealbook.nytimes.com/2010/12/22/hilton-and-starwood-settle-dispute/?_php=true&_type=blogs&_r=0
[21] Jane Hodges, "Though Shalt Not Steal Thy Competitor's Secrets," CBS Money Watch, March 28, 2007, http://www.cbsnews.com/news/thou-shalt-not-steal-thy-competitors-secrets/

Finally, we saw the People's Republic of China push back from allegations that a special computer intelligence unit of the People's Liberation Army had been involved in stealing U.S. trade secrets in the metal and solar businesses by counter-alleging that major U.S. consulting firms such as McKinsey & Company, The Boston Consulting Group on Strategy (formerly Booz & Company) had been providing sensitive business information to the U.S. government on Chinese state-owned and run enterprises. While, in my experience, I did not see the U.S. government trying to get business trade secrets to share with U.S. businesses, I am aware that some U.S. government counterintelligence agencies were talking with American companies trying to determine, from a counterintelligence perspective, which Chinese state-owned enterprises might have been involved in business spying. If you are profiting from committing business espionage, and someone is gathering information on your activities and that could limit what you get from future spying, that could be considered "business spying" but a more accurate term would be "counterespionage" because all that you are sharing with businesses in how to protect information that is already their business/trade secret.[22] What I have seen is consistent with the earlier cited comments from CIA officials that the focus of U.S. government business-information gathering has been counterintelligence oriented.

Then, of course, the U.S. government—like all governments—will not hesitate to gather information that could be of interest for inter-government affairs. For example, the French protested that U.S. intelligence was trying to gather information on France's position relative to the formation of the World Trade Organization. Yet another incident involved the disclosure that American intelligence agents assisted U.S. trade negotiators by eavesdropping on Japanese officials in the cantankerous dispute over car imports. The U.S. Trade Representative at the time, Mickey Kantor and his aides, were the reported beneficiaries of daily briefings by the U.S. intelligence officials, including information gathered by the U.S. National Security Agency's vast electronic network. How useful this information was remains open to debate. After all, the agreement the United States and Japan ultimately reached was hardly an unambiguous victory for the United States.[23]

---

[22] Hilary Russ, "China's state-owned sector told to cut ties with U.S. Consulting firms," Reuters, May 25, 1014, http://www.reuters.com/article/2014/05/25/us-china-cybercrime-consulting-idUSBREA4O0AH20140525

[23] Peter Schweizer, "Growth of Economic Espionage: America is Target Number One," *Foreign Affairs* Magazine, January/February 1996.

It is also worth noting that there are countless cases of ethnic Chinese committing business espionage in the United States. I personally knew an intelligence operative with the Chinese military intelligence community when I was living and working in Beijing. Imagine my surprise when I learned that this female operative and her mother, the widow of a Chinese People's Liberation Army general officer, were living in the United States. I encountered them in a major metropolitan airport in the U.S. and found out they were living in California. Yet another example of how many Chinese spies are living and working inside the U.S.

Vulnerabilities Identified in Examples

First and foremost, employees, especially expatriate managers, were not prepared for the espionage threats they faced in various geographic regions. Certainly the various local employees did not receive adequate and appropriate training on the threats faced. There was no formal education and awareness program, especially prior to or upon arrival in the countries. Likewise, there was no travel security for visitors that would enlighten them on the threats they would face when traveling to these countries. Almost no employees understood the threat faced in hotel rooms, and there was no formal program for reporting possible business espionage.

- A TSCM sweep with TSCM equipment could not be performed for much of this period of time because, for example, the Chinese government forbade it (many of the listening devices were government devices). But a physical examination of properties and areas was also often not conducted and that could still have been accomplished.
- Very few sensitive documents and computer servers, etc., were locked up and well-protected. There was no monitored internal security force and too many times a company relied entirely on office or housing security elements.
- There was a limited security approach for business meetings and little or no education and awareness training on the threats.
- There were an insufficient number of cross-cut shredders and means for destroying sensitive documents and materials available in many instances where trash covers were able to pull out classified or sensitive documents or information. Sensitive documents still ended up in the regular trash too many times and that indicates a problem with security education and awareness and a lack of convenience or enforcement for protecting sensitive information.
- There were sometimes no secure special security areas within the office complex and no areas where cleaning, maintenance,

or security were escorted or otherwise not allowed alone by themselves.

- Security was frequently not a part of the determination of business locations, operations, or meeting locations.
- There was often no TSCM support for important business meetings or activities.
- Aesthetics (for example, having an open view into a scenic garden) too often won out over security and the result was costly compromises.
- Employees were often not bound by non-disclosure requirements and sensitive information was regularly not adequately identified and given high levels of protection and access to information limited to an absolute need-to-know.
- There were incidents where there was clearly incomplete background and other screening required for employees and especially contract service providers such as cleaning staff and security. If required, no one was enforcing compliance with the standards.
- There were often no special security areas within the office complex and no areas where contractors or those without a need-to-know such as cleaning, maintenance, or security were escorted or otherwise not allowed alone by themselves. Even though processes were considered valuable, no one thought about restricting access to staff such as cleaners and security.

Summary

Business espionage threat remains high in Asia—especially in Greater China (People's Republic of China, Taiwan, and Hong Kong SAR)—but there is also a substantial threat in the Republic of Korea, Japan, the Philippines, Singapore, and India. There is a relatively high business-spying threat in Latin America. This includes Cuba, Venezuela, Brazil, and Mexico. Other high-threat regions include Europe where Russia, France, and Germany lead the threat and in the Middle East where the Israelis have the best business-spying effort. Finally, even Africa is contributing to the threat as members of the African Union are joining Zimbabwe and South Africa as new centers of business spying.

The threat can come in many forms and may vary depending on the type of business and the location, but the threat of business spying cannot be ignored anywhere in the world.

Several agencies from various governments have shared their country threat lists with me. By adding situations where I have personally been involved in identifying and countering business spying to this combined list, I have come up with what I term the "Dirty Dozen" list. It includes the 12 highest threat countries when it comes to business-espionage activities. The following is a good list to focus on as the highest threat countries:

1. People's Republic of China (including Hong Kong SAR)
2. Taiwan
3. Japan
4. Republic of Korea
5. India
6. Russia
7. France
8. Israel
9. Vietnam
10. Brazil
11. Venezuela
12. Cuba

According to the Business Action to Stop Counterfeiting and Piracy, British Software Association, and the U.S. Trade Representative report on intellectual property, the 10 countries with the worst intellectual property protection programs are:

1. People's Republic of China
2. Russia
3. Argentina
4. Ukraine
5. Turkey

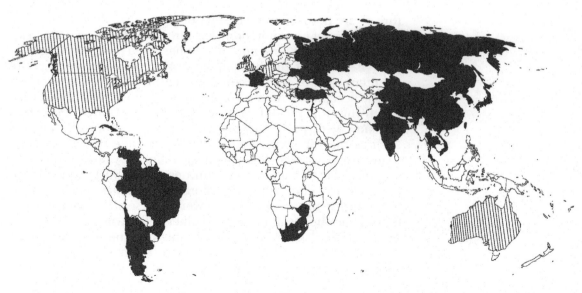

This map highlights the geographic locations with the highest threat countries colored in black. A number of other countries are considered high threat and are marked with hash lines.

6. Venezuela
7. Thailand
8. Lebanon
9. India
10. Chile

These lists are a good start for focusing on geographic-related threats from business espionage. Just because a country is not on the list does not mean there is no business espionage threat there. There are a number of emerging threat countries, so the list is evolving. In fact, if you look at victim countries, the United States would be right at the top of the list even though it has some of the stronger laws relating to business espionage. Two of the biggest threat countries, Russia and the People's Republic of China, have reported spying on each other.

But if you are starting a program, look at business being conducted in the "Dirty Dozen" locations or the lowest intellectual property protection countries and focus there as you begin a risk-based approach because the threat is high in those locations. Once you have calculated the consequences/business impact and have determined any gaps/vulnerabilities in your existing security, the risk ranking may change but this can be a good start. In fact, at least three major companies I have worked with have made changes in plans and do not allow high-consequence sensitive business information into some of these countries precisely because of the simultaneous high threat posed there.

Does this mean that countries that are considered "high threat" are not places to conduct business? No, that is definitely not the correct interpretation of security risk. Just because a location is high threat does not mean it has to be high risk. If a company is aware of the high threat and implements appropriate countermeasures for the consequence/threat, the risk level can still be acceptable. After all, in business there is virtually nothing worthwhile that is risk-free. Likewise, while the United States does not show up on the high-threat list because government programs such as the Espionage Act of 1996 have some deterrent effect, many experts agree that the availability of valuable business secrets in the U.S. and other countries means business spies will continue to conduct espionage there. If companies decide that the lower threat means they can lower their security countermeasures, then the resulting higher vulnerability will mean they will be at higher risk for damaging business-spying incidents when coupled with the high consequences/adverse business conseuqnces they potentially face.

4

ESPIONAGE BY ELECTRONIC MEANS

CHAPTER OUTLINE

Abstract

This chapter includes information on how various electronic means and techniques can be used to copy and steal sensitive business information. This includes case studies where hidden microphones, transmitters, laser beams, key stroke readers, cameras and telephone taps were employed in business spying incidents that occurred around the world. It also discusses how social engineering or insiders were often used to assist in introducing electronic spying devices or access to otherwise sensitive equipment such as IT systems, executive offices or conference rooms.

Introduction

The use of electronic eavesdropping or other electronic penetrations continues at an alarmingly high rate in the world of business spying. This is especially true as miniaturization has improved, allowing for smaller devices and easier concealment within everyday items (such as pens, glasses, ties, etc.). Additionally, what was once the venue of government, spy agencies are now available to anyone in the commercial marketplace. As a result, for most businesses, spy technology continues to outpace security measures. Spies using electronic eavesdropping and

Business Espionage
© 2015 Elsevier Inc. All rights reserved.

other devices are increasingly creative in their espionage efforts. They use the full range of comprehensive techniques and exploit the latest technology to conduct business spying. It is important that counterespionage personnel adjust to these new technologies and approaches. Businesses must educate their staff on how the latest technologies can be exploited, especially when access is given through "insiders" who already have legitimate access to the information or premises. It is also important to understand that technical attacks are also often accompanied by "social engineering." Social engineering is a term that describes a non-technical kind of intrusion where there is human interaction. It often involves "tricking" other people into breaking normal security procedures. Some have linked the term with another term: a "con game." For example, a person using social engineering to break into a computer server might try to gain the confidence of someone authorized to enter the server room and get them to reveal information that compromises the security of the "server room." Social engineers often rely on the natural helpfulness of people as well as on their weaknesses. They might, for example, call the authorized employee with some kind of urgent problem that requires immediate access. It can also include using an appeal to vanity, an appeal to authority, or an appeal to greed. These are all typical social engineering techniques. Social engineering is a component of many, if not most, types of exploits. Virus writers use social engineering tactics to persuade people to run malware-laden email attachments, phishers use social engineering to convince people to divulge sensitive information, and scareware vendors use social engineering to frighten people into running software that is useless at best and dangerous at worst.

In fact, in my experience, the following are the top 10 ways that business spies have been able to install "spyware" that gives them access to sensitive information:

1. Screen savers
2. Emoticons
3. Clip art
4. Spam
5. Email attachments
6. Unprotected web browsing (cookies)
7. Peer-to-Peer applications (mp3 and similar files)
8. Give-away or found thumbdrives
9. Shareware or freeware
10. Involuntary downloads (this may be presented as a fictitious error that you must click on to correct)

Be wary of any of the above. By policy and education/ awareness encourage employees to not use any of the above on company systems and hence give the spies an easy opportunity to install "spyware."

Another method that has been used a number of times is to have employees use a thumbdrive that contains software that introduces a virus into the computer it is inserted into, and potentially into the company's IT system. Two examples of that occurred in Texas and in Colorado in 2004. In one case it was determined that the virus was introduced when an employee found a thumbdrive laying out in the company parking lot and placed it in his computer to try and figure out who it belonged to. In fact, three employees of the company had done the same thing because apparently someone had scattered a dozen or more contaminated thumbdrives in the company parking lot. Another incident occurred when employees attended a trade show. A competitor gave the marketing staff free thumbdrives that had attractive shapes and colors as a gift, but it was later determined that these thumbdrives contained a virus that caused some major problems on the company's IT system. Unfortunately employees were not trained about not inserting these devices into the company's computers.

Electronic eavesdropping is sometimes performed by state-sponsored intelligence agencies on behalf of the government and government-supported competitors. This threat is particularly difficult to deal with because some governments, such as the People's Republic of China, limit the ability of companies to do Technical Surveillance Countermeasures (TSCM) surveys to electronically detect and neutralize electronic eavesdropping devices. Governments also often have access to rooms, telephone boxes, computer servers, and entire systems. But electronic eavesdropping can also be conducted by private, professional intelligence brokers or just individuals using commercially available technology. The spies use this method to gather information of all kinds that could potentially have some business value. This includes data on legal cases, formulas and sales strategies, personal data, computer data, telephone conversations, business documents, finance documents, public relations, communication with corporate headquarters, friends and family data, bidding and pricing as well as strategic planning and goals.

The examples that follow took place between the mid-1990s and the present in South Africa, the Philippines, Taiwan, Hong Kong SAR, Germany, Australia/Canada, the United States, and the United Kingdom and illustrate a number of different eavesdropping methods or other electronic-spying techniques.

Cases of Electronic Eavesdropping

Over a period of years, going back to the late 1990s and into the twenty-first century, there have been a number of incidents involving electronic eavesdropping or the use of the latest technology to surreptitiously gather sensitive business information.

In one recent (late 2013) incident, a company in South Africa had some very valuable cargo that was being transported by truck on a regular basis. As that cargo traveled, it was becoming more and more common for armed robbers to successfully stop and hold up the driver. Even though security measures got more and more sophisticated, using, for example, multiple decoy vehicles, the "bad guys" did not seem to be falling for it. No one confronted any of the decoys and the cargo escort was successfully attacked multiple times. Measures were being taken to restrict knowledge of which vehicles had the cargo and which were decoys because it was believed there was a high likelihood that an insider was responsible for helping the robbers identify the vehicle with the valuable cargo.

Early on, when the robberies were becoming commonplace, the senior manager of the company made the comment to colleagues that a bird was building a nest or seemed to like resting by his window on an upper floor of the company's headquarters. Everyone laughed as the bird hovered outside his window during meetings to discuss the robberies. Then one day, some members of his staff brought a strange device into the office. It looked like a dead bird except when the stomach area of the bird was lifted up, the "bird" was stuffed with a camera and electronics, including a microphone. The company maintenance staff had found it lying on the ground, having apparently malfunctioned and crashed within the company's fenced and heavily protected compound. The "bird" was, in fact, a remote-controlled drone that was being used to photograph and eavesdrop. It was this means that was used to gather information. The company had extensive traditional physical security: walls/fences, gates, lighting, CCTV, locks, access control, armed security guards, etc., but security personnel had never even considered protecting the actions and conversations of managers and planners from an external drone/unmanned aerial vehicle (UAV).

In another incident in approximately 1998, in the Philippines, a dairy company suffered a number of lost contracts. The dairy company was being consistently underbid. The company began to reverse engineer its pricing and approach to try and refine its strategy. But whenever they made adjustments, their principal competitor apparently adjusted too and they were still losing.

At this point, management realized they might have a different kind of problem—perhaps an internal source was feeding the competition information. They redoubled efforts to closely protect bid information and confine everything to a closed and guarded "work center" conference room. Still the problems persisted. Finally, legal counsel advised them to consider a TSCM sweep. As the TSCM team worked through the office area they found nothing, but when they checked the PBX (public telephone exchange) room, a recording device was found attached to their office telephone lines. It was determined that their competitors had paid Philippine National Police officers to come into the office building, show their identification to building security officers, and thus gain access to the PBX where they sat up telephone tap equipment, which was both recorded and transmitted.

In another incident, this time in Taiwan in approximately 1996, a U.S. missile systems and military equipment manufacturing firm had an office in Taipei. Unbeknownst to them, a French competitor firm rented an office immediately above the U.S. company's conference room area. After a number of incidents that included allegations that the French company was paying people to ride the elevators and listen to business-related conversations in the elevators, a TSCM sweep was requested. The covert sweep found there were multiple microphones lowered, through the air conditioning ducts within the building, from the French company's office space into the U.S. firm's conference room and adjacent office areas.

Another example occurred in the early twenty-first century and affected a Western firm that maintained an office in Beijing, China. The contract cleaning crew had keys to enter every office, including that of the country president. No one monitored the cleaning staff while they were in any areas including senior executive's offices and sensitive areas such as the research and development lab and the server room. At some point, the company expressed concern about the leaking of sensitive information. The company president said that some of the information that had somehow been leaked went back to private conversations he had on the telephone or in his office. My team was called in to do a thorough review. It began with a physical search since a formal TSCM sweep could not be performed. The initial check of telephones did not disclose any issues within the office and building phone system, but later on our technical specialist detected a possible problem on the president's desk. The president was briefed off-site and he did not discuss anything at his desk that day. Covert cameras were installed in his office and several hours after he left for the day, a contract cleaner came into his office and retrieved a pen from his pen holder on his desk. The cleaner appeared to replace the pen with another identical pen. When we checked the pen we discovered a microphone and recording capability were built-in as part of the pen. The company president was shocked because he said the pen was almost exactly like the original pen set that he had brought with him from his home country. When the cleaner was confronted the next night while switching pens again, he confessed that he was being paid extra by an individual who paid him daily to remove the pen and give it back to the pen provider. The handler would then give the cleaner a newly charged pen to replace in the desk pen holder.

In Hong Kong SAR, in approximately 1998, a Hong Kong soft drink and bottling company was experiencing problems with a new competitor. Once again, the soft drink company complained that its new competitor seemed to know their business strategies before they were even implemented and made plans to effectively counter their strategies. When I asked about where their strategic planning took place, the management acknowledged that some parts of it were developed in multiple departments but it was always presented in a comprehensive meeting that was held twice a year in their main conference room. I suggested we start with a TSCM sweep of the conference room and then move to department heads offices. Within 30 minutes of initiating the sweep, our TSCM expert had uncovered a transmitter wired into electric sockets in the conference room and also detected a laser apparently being used to monitor vibrations on the unprotected windows of the conference room from an adjacent building.

Another electronic-spying incident took place in Hong Kong in 1999 when an accounting firm was struggling with a similar type of competitive business entity for contracts within the People's Republic of China. Several of their employees had left and joined this new business and were successfully competing with their old firm. The accounting firm management brought in their contract legal counsel to discuss the situation and one of the partners made the comment, "It's like they are sitting right here with us and know our every strategy and move." The attorney had attended a business espionage presentation that included some examples of covert "bugs," including a calculator that was a listening device with a built-in transmitter. He suggested to his clients that the problem might be business spying. As he was speaking, he saw a calculator on the conference room table and picked it up, noting that the device he saw at the presentation had a small hole where the microphone was located. When he realized the calculator that had been on the conference room table had the same small holes he had seen in the presentation, he immediately left the conference room and the rest of the company staff "evacuated" too. A TSCM sweep was ordered and it was confirmed that the calculator did contain a hidden microphone and transmitter. The sweep also found two more transmitters wired into and hidden in electric sockets in the room. A subsequent investigation determined that, ironically, the devices used for spying had been purchased on a company credit card by an employee who left. They bought the devices and undoubtedly installed them prior to resigning and leaving. Once they were working with the new firm, they used the devices to get "insider" information from their old firm and exploit it in the competitive bidding process.

Getting pricing and competitive bidding information was the driving force for yet another electronic espionage matter that took place in northern Australia in 2010. In this case, an Australian mining company was regularly running into problems with computer hackers who were targeting their computers and those of their law firms in Canada. The apparent objective of the alleged Chinese-based hackers was to find a way to stop an acquisition bid for a major potash mine in Canada. Apparently the Australian company's computer system was reasonably well protected so the hackers chose to target several law firms retained by the Australian company because the law firms' computer systems were an easier target.

Many people, in business, and outside of it, love technology. Whenever a new technology is introduced, many people will jump on the opportunity to use it. In 2013, a technology company in the U.S. introduced a new office cleaning solution. Instead of relying on janitorial staff to run vacuum cleaners, brooms, and mops, this company relied on a series of robotic cleaners that were guided by cameras and directed by electronic transmissions. One American firm, located within the U.S., was delighted with this new high-tech cleaning solution and the money they would save on contract janitorial services. The devices would move around the offices within the building and cleaning away. Office staff became used to the cleaning robots and soon carried on business activities and conversations as if the robots were another piece of office furniture. However, after competitors repeatedly released competing products and services just ahead of their projected roll-outs, the company leadership began to think about the fact that some employees might be giving information to the competition. During one of the meetings, a cleaning robot was unobtrusively moving across the floor when one of the executives had an epiphany and picked up the device. He asked if anyone knew where the camera transmissions were going. A security assessment of the cleaning robot determined it was both providing video and audio of what was happening around it. Needless to say, that was the end of that company allowing surreptitious cleaning devices within its premises during business hours and operations. But how many more companies have these high-tech robots taking them to the "cleaners?"

In the same general time frame, a U.S. business leader and family were living in Berlin, Germany. One afternoon when he was home, two very attractive females knocked on the door of the residence. They used "social engineering" and had a cover story about being lost and trying to find a friend's residence. They acted surprised that the American did not speak fluent German but they quickly began speaking in fluent English. They asked if they could use the individual's home telephone to make a local call to their friend. They verified the address they were at and appeared to be getting directions. After the completed the call, they apologized for bothering the individual, got into their vehicle and left. The American was suspicious and I was able to help him by doing a TSCM sweep team to see if the two women had planted any listening devices, as he suspected. None were found, however, subsequently it was discovered that someone—the government or private individuals hired to do so—had placed a recorder on the line at a juncture box not far from the residence. It was then apparent that the individual had successfully detected social engineering and that his suspicions were well founded. The pretext call had just been to ensure that the spies had the correct home telephone number and could record from the telephone system juncture box.

In 2013 it was reported that eight men in London, England (United Kingdom) were accused of using social engineering to get past a receptionist and then install a keyboard video mouse (KVM) on Barclays Bank and Santander Bank computer systems that allowed them to get information that, in turn, was used to steal millions of dollars from the banks. News reports said the men were able to convince bank personnel that they were engineers there to do some maintenance on the banks' computers. When bank staff let them have unimpeded and unmonitored access to the computers, they were able to install a KVM on the computers and steal passwords and data that enabled them to, in turn, steal information and money.[1]

While this next example is not an electronic eavesdropping technique, per se, it is a situation when a business spy used the latest technology and exploited social networks for business espionage purposes. It is an example that shows how business spies

---

[1] "8 Arrested in Cybertheft of Barclays Branch," *Tampa Tribune*, September 21, 2013.

are increasingly turning to social networks (e.g., Linked-In, Face-book, etc.) to assist them with business spying and, given the popularity of such networks, it is important for employers and employees to understand how these networks can be used to further business-spying efforts.

In early 2013, a large global retail firm was engaged in competition with a Korean firm for access to tourist markets in Singapore and elsewhere in Asia. Suddenly their personnel started getting unusual contact requests on social media such as LinkedIn and Facebook. The gist of the communication (which was determined to have been generated by a German consulting firm) was that the retail firm's employees had been identified as "having demonstrated outstanding expertise in their field" of business. The consulting firm said it wanted to do some research on how they conducted business. The firm then said they would hire these individuals as outside consultants and pay them for their expertise and advice. Of course, the questions they asked and the information they wanted would require the employee to give up sensitive proprietary information about their current employer. That information would then be of great benefit to the Korean firm in the competitive bidding process. Additionally, senior staff members started getting invitations to expensive dinners from former employees who were known to be affiliated with the Korean competitor. These former employees suddenly reached out to the company's counterparts and wanted to talk about how business was going. Once again, the questions were such that any answer would help the Korean firm to construct a competitive bid.

Another use of technology for electronic eavesdropping/spying has to do with the way the latest, now digital, printers, faxes, and copiers work. In 2000, a U.S. high-technology firm, located on the West Coast of the U.S. called me t reported a security concern. After meeting with the firm's management, a story about using social engineering and exploiting technology for business spying emerged. It seems that an individual arrived at the front desk of the company (an engineering firm) that morning and claimed to be there to service their combination copier/printer. The individual had the uniform of the company that did the preventive maintenance on the equipment. When the administrator at the front desk asked where the usual service technician was, the individual said he was on vacation. He proceeded to the copier/printer, serviced it, and left. Later that afternoon, on the same day, the usual technician arrived and said he was there to service the machine. The administrator told him that she thought he was on vacation. "I wish!" was his reply. He asked why she thought that and she told him that someone else from his company had been by that morning and already did the servicing. After a few surprising phone calls it was clear that whoever had serviced the machine was not from the legitimate service company. The technician did advise the company that whoever it was who had been there in the morning had removed the machine's digital hard drive (which could hold up to 10,000 images of the last documents copied or printed) and left a brand new, clean drive in its place. Interestingly, the engineering firm was in the final stages of a very competitive bid and much of the information that would have been printed in the past days would have been related to that bid. They ultimately lost the bid to a competitor firm based primarily on pricing. This use of social engineering and using technology to steal business secrets has been repeated over and over again.

Another time we were conducting a TSCM sweep at a company's office in Hong Kong. The company had been having some business issues that made them wonder if they were being spied on by competitors. We were there at night since the company did not want anyone to know they were conducting the sweep. While doing a telephone check one of our staff heard a telephone ring in another office. The team moved toward that office and noticed that it was the fax machine and it was engaged. However, no one was faxing anything to the office and there obviously was no employee there faxing something out. A careful examination of the machine determined that someone was calling the fax machine at night and was able to download all of the data on the equipment's hard drive. The original purpose of that feature was to allow the company that leased the equipment to do preventive maintenance, but it also had an obvious vulnerability if the access program was abused and, in this case, it was indeed being exploited.

But just plain carelessness can also a result in a compromise from the hard drives of digital copiers and printers. A good example of this was a story initially reported by CBS Evening News in 2010. Reporters went to a huge warehouse in New Jersey where they found more than 6000 used copiers being stored for resale. Container loads of them were on their way to Asia and Latin America. The reporters bought several of the machines for US$300 each and then had a forensic expert retrieve the data on the hard drives. The amount of sensitive information that was on those machines was incredible, ranging from business plans, financial data, medical and personal information, drawings, and even sensitive police informant records.[2] Every day companies are returning printers

---

[2] Armen Keteyian, "Digital Photocopiers Loaded With Secrets," CBS Evening News, April 19, 2010.

and copiers that they leased or are buying new equipment and are turning in their old equipment. The question everyone should be asking is: What is going to happen to the information stored on those machine's digital hard drives? Is any of it sensitive? But this is just not happening, and I cringe every time I see someone carting these devices off.

Vulnerabilities Identified

First and foremost, employees, especially expatriates in foreign countries, were usually not prepared for the espionage threats they faced in these locations. There was no formal education and awareness program, especially prior to arrival in the foreign country. Likewise, there was no travel security for visitors that would enlighten them on the threats they would face when traveling in the United States, Europe, Asia, or Africa. Almost no employee understood the threat faced in offices, and there was no formal program for reporting possible business espionage. Security personnel were also not trained on the latest threats from business espionage and looked at protective security measures only from a traditional physical security standpoint. Few employees in companies understand these electronic threats and the important role social engineering can play in the electronic penetrations.

Additionally:

- A TSCM sweep could not be performed in China from 1998 onward because the Chinese government forbade, and continues to forbid it, since many of the listening devices uncovered during the process are government devices. But a physical examination of properties and areas was also not conducted and that could have been accomplished. TSCM sweeps can be accomplished in most venues but were not a part of any incidents until after the fact.
- Those responsible for security are too set in ways and never seem to be ready for the latest threats. They might do a TSCM sweep but no one looks up or has the capability to look for a drone. High-tech robotic cleaners are a cool new technology, but no one thinks of them as a potential spy. Social media is popular in the twenty-first century, but few realize that it also provides a good way to assess and recruit both witting and unwitting spies. Therefore, few companies train people about that threat and monitor or test employees.
- Very few sensitive documents and computer servers, etc., were locked up and protected in an effective manner. There was often no monitored internal security force and too often

companies relied entirely on office building or housing complex security—regardless of their loyalties or lack thereof.

- There was often a limited security protocol for business meetings and little or no education and awareness training on the potential business espionage threats that might be faced.
- There were rarely special security areas within the office complex, areas where cleaning, maintenance, or security were escorted or otherwise not allowed alone by themselves. High-consequence areas should require such an escort.
- Vulnerabilities must extend to anyone who might have your sensitive information including business partners, law firms, accounting firms, etc. You can reduce your company's vulnerabilities but you must also require the same standards of protection from any other individual or firm that has access to your sensitive information.
- In the twenty-first century it is important to have good IT security and to remember its link to effective physical security measures.
- Employees are rarely educated and trained on the threats posed by social media and postings on those venues. The same is true for threats posed by printers/copiers and their digital memory or the ability to dial into those linked to telephone or computer lines and download memory, ostensibly for maintenance purposes.
- Staff is unaware that sensitive information remains on any copy machine or printer produced after approximately 2002. Repair personnel should be monitored and no hard drive should be allowed to be removed until the company insures no sensitive information can be obtained from it.

Summary

The diversity of electronic espionage methods available for use by business spies means it is a significant part of the overall business espionage threat. Additionally, the use of electronic devices and means is constantly evolving as technology improves. It is important to keep this threat in mind as companies determine how to protect their business secrets and develop counterespionage countermeasures.

5

ESPIONAGE BY FORCE: PHYSICAL THEFT OR OTHER APPROPRIATION

Abstract

This chapter includes information on how good, old-fashioned force and theft can result in loss of sensitive business information to business spies. Techniques include theft of prototypes, documents, processes, trash, and computers. Examples of this take place around the world where poor understanding of the business espionage threats and techniques, poor education and awareness training and poor physical security make business spying entirely too easy.

Introduction

Physically breaking into buildings, vehicles, offices, and homes to steal information such as documents or equipment and digital electronic devices such as laptops, iPads, and iPhones is another technique used over and over again by business spies. There are also other methods that involve physically gaining access to sensitive information without an actual "break-in." This includes the recruitment of insiders who have legitimate access to information or planting individuals on the inside (we will address this in more detail in Chapter 6). It might come in the form of business partners who have otherwise legitimate access to some information. It may involve something like trash covers, also known as "dumpster diving" or "raiding the black forest." This is a widely used technique in business espionage and it occurs when business spies sort through trash to find individual bits of sensitive business information.

Unfortunately, too often break-ins and thefts are thought to be criminal acts to steal equipment when, in fact, they are acts of business espionage and the equipment is stolen in order to get access to the information stored on the devices. Some companies also mistakenly believe that there is nothing of value in a company's trash and that no one would steal it. Other companies find it hard to believe that one of their employees or business partners would betray them.

Physical theft of property is known to be performed both by state-sponsored intelligence agencies on behalf of the government and government-supported competitors, as well as private, professional intelligence brokers or individuals. Using the stolen devices, spies are able to gather information of all kinds that could potentially have some business value, such as data on legal cases, formulas and sales strategies, personal data, computer data, business documents, finance documents, bidding and pricing as well as strategic planning and goals.

The following examples of physical theft or other appropriation took place between the mid-1990s and the present, in China, Taiwan, Korea, Singapore, India, Mexico, Brazil, and the U.S. and involve entities from these regions as well as Europe. These examples show how individuals can break into offices, hotels, and residences or otherwise steal information of value. Many times the victims of the overt theft think they were just unlucky. In reality, they often are targets of business espionage. The culprit's goal was not the device in and of itself, but the information on the device or information about devices the company is working to create.

Cases of Business Espionage by Physical Theft or Other Appropriation

In addition to the examples that were described as taking place in China, there are some other examples of break-ins that illustrate this method is widely used in business spying. Over a period of years, going back to the late 1990s and into the twenty-first century, there have been a number of incidents involving outright break-ins and theft or appropriation of sensitive information from offices, homes, and other locations.

In one incident that occurred in 1999, a toy manufacturing company executive was attending a toy show in Taipei, Taiwan. As a part of the marketing for his company, he brought several prototypes to the show and revealed them at the booth. Because they were still prototypes, he did not allow them to be examined but did expose them to his potential marketplace. After the final day of the show, he brought the prototypes back to his home and kept them at his residence overnight. His plan was to take his family to dinner and return the prototypes to the office the next day. When he returned home with his family after dinner, they found someone had broken into their house. A window had been broken and someone had unlocked the door after climbing in through it. An examination of the house determined that the only thing missing was the prototype toys. When he went to the office the next day, he was told that during the previous night someone had apparently broken into the office by prying open the door lock but nothing was missing. The company speculated that someone first broke into the office and when they did not find anything, they located the executive's house and broke in there. Less than six months later, a competitor company came out with toys very similar to the prototypes and it took the company another four months to fully recreate another set of prototypes.

In Guangdong Province, People's Republic of China in 1999, a firm that was renowned for their dim sum in Hong Kong SAR decided to move some of their dim sum manufacturing process over the border into mainland China. They took both their recipes and their processes into China in an effort to cut costs. Suddenly a new firm emerged that seemed to have the same ingredients, taste, and look of the firm's famous dim sum. Previous efforts to compete had failed as the product produced in China was not of the same quality as the Hong Kong company's dim sum. But this was different. The new competitive dim sum came only six months after the company began production on the mainland. After we did an in-depth investigation it was determined that some of the new competition's executives were family members of existing employees in their Guangdong facility. It became obvious that trusted members of the manufacturing facility had betrayed the trust of the Hong Kong-based company and had exploited the open access to customer lists, recipes, and the manufacturing processes that had been allowed at the new site.

A U.S.-headquartered furniture manufacturer outsourced some furniture making to China in 2011. The Chinese company they worked with allegedly stole their plans and designs and undercut the price of furniture sold by the U.S. company. Within two years of sharing plans and designs with their "partner" in

China they saw copies of their furniture showing up on the U.S. market, in direct competition.[1]

In Singapore in 2002, a firm that manufactured portable toilets and sold them throughout Asia called to report that a firm was contacting their customers in the construction business and were offering comparable portable toilets at slightly lower prices. In the past couple of weeks, the competitor company had started to contact customers for temporary events. The company became convinced that the competitor company was somehow stealing their information. As we reviewed the company's existing countermeasures it became apparent that the company had done nothing to protect its sensitive information on manufacturing specifications, processes, and even customer lists. Once again, after the fact, an investigation determined that the competing company was owned by relatives of some of their employees; it wasn't long before these employees resigned and overtly began working for their relatives at the new company. It was clear that the lack of concern about protecting sensitive information had made it easy for a competitor to spring up. When the company attempted to put together a legal case in Singapore, the new company moved its operations to the People's Republic of China and began competing from there. It was determined that there was little other recourse at that point in time.

In another incident in approximately 2008, a law firm was victimized in California. The theft was sophisticated because it involved social engineering and distraction, along with theft. The law firm was involved in an extensive litigation case. One morning, just before a critical filing, the receptionist was at her desk and the phone rang. Someone began swearing at her and screaming. As she tried to figure out who the caller was and what they wanted, an individual walked into the lobby. He came up to the reception desk and started asking about a neighboring building. As the receptionist tried to give him directions, the person on the telephone began screaming more loudly. As the receptionist tried to calm down the caller, the individual standing at her desk escalated his questioning and demanded she give him her attention as he was late for an appointment. While she juggled with these conflicting priorities, a third individual dressed in a suit and with a briefcase, walked past her desk and into the office area where attorneys and staff have their offices. The receptionist tried to stop him but he just waved and smiled and she was forced to deal with the most pressing "threats" from the other two

---

[1] Steve Dickinson, *China Law Blog*, March 27, 2012, http://www.chinalawblog.com/about.

individuals. The nicely dressed man apparently went directly to the unlocked office of the attorney responsible for the big case and removed the laptop from the desk of the lead attorney. He then went into an adjoining office and the cubicles outside of the offices. A total of four laptops were removed. Unfortunately there were no backups and the loss of the information was of value to their opponent in the legal action and it also slowed down their case, which they ultimately lost because the judge said, among other things, that the law firm took too long to prepare the case.

In 2008, a large international software company believed its research and development (R & D) offices in Shanghai, China were being subjected to penetrations and theft of information. Initially the company could not figure out how they were losing information but, because of competitor actions, it became apparent that sensitive R & D information was somehow being compromised. The company conducted extensive physical security assessments looking at traditional access controls (doors, locks, keys, etc.) and could not find a single vulnerability. Additionally, they worked with building security to check CCTV coverage of the outside doors into their office area. Rigorous reviews of the CCTV coverage uncovered nothing that indicated someone was entering their facilities without authorization. Finally, a security/investigations company was retained that installed covert cameras on the doors into the R & D area and inside the R & D work area. About 10 p.m. on successive nights, several individuals were seen on camera, manipulating the lock and entering the R & D area. Covert cameras within the R & D area then showed this team of people going through items, copying white boards and notes, taking photographs, and downloading from computers. Access control records and contact alarm records for all doors showed the doors were not opened prior to the penetrating team appearing on the covert cameras. The security/investigative team then did an exhaustive vulnerability assessment examining every door, window, vent, etc. In the women's restroom, located within the office area, a security specialist found a door that appeared to only access water and waste water pipes. But after an extraordinarily detailed and thorough examination, it was determined that there was another door on the backside of the compartment for the pipes and it opened into an unknown office on the same floor. Ultimately additional covert systems determined that the spies were using this physical "back door" to access the software company's R & D area, which had weak protection because their main protection was focused on the office area's outer perimeter and the company had convinced itself this was sufficient.

Social engineering and theft or loss of information is often linked because social engineering can enable a spy to get inside a facility and wander around. Social engineering is a term that became popular a number of years ago when Kevin Mitnick used the term to describe how hackers tell lies over a telephone, or in person, to get information.[2] It reflects how individuals can use their social skills to elicit information or "schmooze" their way into a facility. In 1998, I met an individual in Taiwan and he admitted to me that he had been sent to a U.S. computer firm in Taipei to try and determine the customers of the company. He related that he found out the company had some open positions so he went through human resources and applied for a position using some fictitious information for name/address/skills and experience. While filling out the application and being interviewed by human resources, he asked if he could use the restroom. After HR directed him to the restroom, he diverted to the mailroom. There, in the open and unsecured mailroom, he told me he found a complete mailing list of customers lying on the counter. He took that and the fax numbers on the bulletin board above the common fax machine. With that information he was able to assemble many of the key clients and suppliers the company used. He then returned to the HR area and no one had detected anything. He said it was obvious that no one was sensitized to the techniques he used and the threat he posed.

Social engineering is especially valuable when working against sales teams. In 1998 I was hired by a U.S. firm to determine if a Chinese competitor had stolen some of their proprietary information and was planning to launch a competing product. After we determined that their concern was legitimate we agreed to accept the assignment. Our approach was to go to the competitor and claim to want to talk about a multi-million dollar purchase. When the sales people heard the amount they were obviously excited (big commissions come from multi-million dollar sales!). We began by asking about the latest capabilities they had (we were extensively trained on what the latest technology was). At one point, it was obvious that they were nervous about sharing this information. But finally, the lead salesman asked his colleagues to leave. He then told us that we were asking questions about something they had not yet formally released but the release was imminent. He said it was still sensitive but very shortly they would be able to meet our needs. When we asked about some key specifications that would

[2] Ira Winkler, *Corporate Espionage*, Prima Publishing, 1997.

indicate this competitor was using stolen information, he said he would not be authorized to release that information, but he told us that the specifications were in a folder he was going to leave on the table. He said he was going to go to the restroom and if we looked in the folder, that was our business. He then winked and left. Sure enough, the specifications and details we needed were in the folder marked "confidential." The head of the sales department was so keen on making this big sale that he gave up sensitive information. All we had to do was effectively be viewed as a genuine potential customer.

This was not unusual and happens again and again. Once in 2004, in Colorado, I was asked by a firm to determine if a former partner, whom had been bought out and who had a non-compete, was, in fact, competing against his former company in violation of his agreement. The firm was an aerospace engineering firm and, after determining their concern was legitimate, I launched an effort to learn the truth. I told the firm that I would approach their competitor with a multi-million dollar project and would structure it in a manner where if the individual was indeed working with them, they would include his resume in their proposal. As I explained my approach, one of my client partners visibly shuddered and shook his head. I asked if there was a problem with my plan and his answer was, "No. In fact, I just realized that if you walked in and requested that of me, I would give you a proposal response, no questions asked." I approached the firm and told them I had a request for a proposal (RFP) that would be millions of dollars and laid it out. The front company I used (and the entire project) was totally made up and fictional, but this company expended considerable efforts putting together the RFP response by the deadline. When I received their nearly 100-page response, sure enough, the individual who supposedly fell under a non-compete was listed among their team. However, attorneys told me that was not enough evidence, since the individual could claim he had no knowledge that his name had been added to a competitor bid. I had to establish that the individual's resume was knowingly included in the package so I told the company I needed to interview their proposed six-person team because I was seriously considering hiring them. I interviewed all six, including the individual who supposedly was under a non-compete, and it was clear that he knowingly was participating in this RFP and knew that his former company was also a competitor. That sealed the case. Time and time again, I see how easily companies can be persuaded to give up information when there is a large "carrot" dangling in front of them. Sales staff are not adequately trained to be alert for business spying and to conduct a full due diligence before releasing any information or pricing.

On another occasion, in 2002, the security office of a large multinational company in Houston, Texas, USA, called for assistance. It seems that one of their senior vice presidents frequently worked from home. When he was in the office, he controlled his sensitive waste by ensuring it was shredded at least daily. He said he "felt" that he was safe at home, however, because he thought no one would know where he lived. One morning, after setting the trash out by the front gate of his home, he was checking on some new plants and noticed a car parked by his trash. Someone had opened the black trash bag and was going through papers he had thrown away, but not shredded. The vice president yelled at the individuals who then just took the trash bag and jumped in their vehicle and drove off. As they drove away, he noted the color and license plate number. The vehicle was subsequently identified as belonging to the French Consulate in Houston and the plates were issued, by the United States Office of Foreign Missions, to an individual whom U.S. authorities told me they believed was a French intelligence officer.

Another incident, in 2003, occurred when an individual from North Carolina went to Norristown, PA, USA, and targeted a bakery there that specialized in making delicious rolls and hoagies. The business spy was able to get into a changing room, steal a company laboratory coat, and then walk around the bakery and video the processes. He also allegedly stole a three-ring binder that contained 66 secret recipes. The business spy, who owned his own bakery in North Carolina, also tried to purchase one of the machines the Norristown bakery used and tried to recruit one of the Norristown bakers to come down and show the spy how to use the equipment and turn the recipes into rolls. In the subsequent legal action, the bakery claimed the recipes had a value of more than US$30 million, but the binder holding the recipes was so poorly protected that the spy easily removed it by just wearing the "uniform" of the bakery.[3]

I have used a similar technique a number of times doing penetration testing and frequently found that if I wore a dark suit and tie, and carried a clipboard, or if I wore a lab coat or other attire that was common in the facility, or wore the attire that potentially signaled a manger at a facility, I could get virtual free rein within the complex and would rarely be challenged.

[3] Michael Currie Schaffer, "Local Baker Says Rival Stole His Bread and Butter," *Philadelphia Inquirer,* July 1, 2003.

Another company called me and expressed concern about an apparent cyber-security issue in India in 1999. It seems that a local Indian competitor had so much knowledge about clients and pricing that it was, in their opinion, obvious the competitor had somehow managed to gain access to actual sensitive client data maintained on their servers. After a thorough review of cyber-security measures turned up no major vulnerabilities, a more comprehensive assessment determined that the data was actually being printed out once a month. When new data was received, the voluminous printouts were taken to the basement of the corporate headquarters for destruction. After talking with the in-house janitorial staff it was determined that several months earlier a man came by and offered them a nice amount of money to take scrap paper off their hands. Since they were holding the printouts for a recycling company that was being paid to make a pickup, the staff thought this was a good way to supplement the company "party fund" by allowing a recycling firm that would give them some money to take the scrap paper rather than pay someone to haul it off. Countersurveillance on the scrap-paper pickups determined that the "recycling" firm was actually a private investigative firm that was working for a major competitor. These scrap printouts were very valuable to the competitor firm, and there was no need for a cyber penetration when the data was available as unprotected scrap at low cost.

While I was working in Hong Kong in 1998, I gave a presentation on business spying at a business association meeting. After the meeting, a member of a local television station came up to talk. He expressed an interest in the topic but said he just did not believe that at the dawn of the twenty-first century, with shredders so readily available, that people still would go through a company's trash to try and come up with sensitive data. I assured him it was happening. He challenged me and asked if I would take some trash on camera and go through it on camera with his news crew. I agreed but he wanted to make certain I did not "seed" the trash (put hand-picked documents into the trash) so he insisted that he be the one to pick the target building in downtown Kowloon in Hong Kong. I told him that was not how a trash cover worked in terms of planning and preparation, but he insisted and I finally relented because I believed it could help educate the public. That next evening I met with the reporter and his camera crew. We went to a building he had selected and found the trash in bins in the basement. With some colleagues from my office, we removed five bags of discarded trash and took them to our office. As we began going through the remnants of lunch boxes and soggy tea bags we were able to determine that four of the five bags had come from a large-chain restaurant headquarters in Hong Kong. During the course of opening the bags I had commented that sometimes people would tear up sensitive information before they threw it into the trash so I always looked for that first and would try and tape the pieces together because that indicated someone thought it was important enough to tear up. Sure enough, we found several documents that had been torn up. While assembling them we found a complete customer list of tour companies that stopped at the restaurants, an income and expense listing for each of the chain's restaurants in Hong Kong, bank statements, and human resources data that included the Hong Kong ID numbers of employees (in violation of the Hong Kong data protection laws). We also found an entire box of canceled checks and bank data. When we assembled the torn documents we found it was (only) the projected specials on the menu for the coming week at each restaurant. So, in this case, the torn-up documents were hardly the most sensitive data in the trash, but that is often not the case. The reporter was astounded that all of that information was just in one day's random snatch of trash bags and the story was on the evening news. While we honorably destroyed the data from the restaurant chain, and this was not true business espionage, it did vividly demonstrate how vulnerable a business can be if they do not do something to protect sensitive information from ending up in the open trash.

On another occasion, in 2001, I was asked to determine if a major corporate headquarters in Omaha, Nebraska, USA, had any sensitive documents that were getting into the regular trash where they could be recovered by competitors. As the cleaning staff gathered the trash from the regular trash containers in the various offices, in cubicles and the mailrooms on each floor, they would take them to the basement where they were picked up by the city. I assembled a team that put on coveralls and rubber gloves and went through every trash container and looked at everything put into the trash. Over the course of several days we found sensitive information in the form of notes and personnel information, even financial documents. A number of the documents were incomplete but what was in the trash was clearly marked "confidential" and "proprietary" and included sensitive documents from every single division in the corporate headquarters, including the CEO's office. After the results of the study, the CEO said he never wanted to do that kind of a study again because the fallout was shocking and would require time-consuming follow-up. When he finally did agree the problem needed to be addressed, major remedial efforts work put in place, including adding more cross-cut shredders, educating the workforce, and assigning security the responsibility of screening the trash for any obvious and marked sensitive information/materials.

In 2012 an international firm had a manufacturing site near Monterrey, Mexico. One morning, as two managers pulled out of a gated housing area, their car was cut off by a vehicle in front of them, which suddenly slammed on the brakes causing them to rear-end the car. A second vehicle, which had been following, pulled up behind and rammed their vehicle from behind. Armed individuals climbed out of both vehicles and took them prisoner. After hoods were placed over their heads and they were tied up, they were taken to a remote back road where an individual began questioning them about their manufacturing processes and how to properly run some manufacturing equipment. The individuals were forced, at gun point, to reveal manufacturing trade secrets. This is a case where physical security clearly was linked to loss of information that, in turn, was related to a competitive advantage.

In 2012, in Brazil, an energy company was surprised to find that when they went to negotiate an acquisition, the company being considered seemed to have knowledge of their pricing and the maximum amount that would be offered. Naturally, the energy company had hoped the pricing would be lower but as the negotiations went on, it was apparent they would have to pay the maximum price, which was approximately US$3 million more than the company had planned on. Executives were puzzled at the way the negotiations proceeded and asked us to look into the employees of the company who had access to the bidding information. As the investigation got underway, one of the administrators resigned and left the company on short notice. We focused on him and determined the individual had suddenly come up with the Brazilian currency equivalent of more than a quarter million U.S. dollars. It was determined that the administrator had sat in on the planning meetings and had prepared some of the confidential acquisition bid documents. Subsequent investigation established that money had been transferred from the owners of the acquired company to this former administrator, which still left the owners of the acquired company with US $2.75 million more than they probably would have gotten without the insider information. It's no wonder why they were willing to pay for it.

Exploiting plant or facility tours is another technique regularly used by business spies. A rather infamous incident occurred in the U.S. in the 1990s when a German engineer was visiting a chemical facility and during a tour "accidently" dipped his tie into a tray containing a liquid. He supposedly declined to throw the tie away since it was a "family gift," but the company later determined that a good analysis of the tie could have compromised some business research secrets.[4] Being familiar with that story, I was surprised in 2000 when representatives from a Japanese company were allowed to go on a tour of its U.S. competitor. While on the tour, one of the Japanese executives "accidently" got his jacket sleeve in a chemical that experts later said could have given them some insight into sensitive research and development underway at the facility. History repeats itself sometimes.

I was also involved, from time-to-time, in school activities at the Taipei American School in Taipei, Taiwan in 1996. At one point during the school year, one of the American manufacturers who had facilities in the Hsin Shu Industrial Park offered to allow third graders to come to their facility and do a tour. It was always interesting when a business executive from a competitor, who never seemed to have time to do anything at the school, called me and volunteered to be a chaperone for the class (his son was in the class). When I realized he was a competitor, I thanked him and told him we did not need any additional chaperones but found it very interesting that the only time he volunteered to do anything at school was when we were doing a tour of his competitor's manufacturing processes.

One of the more bizarre exploitations of "tours" occurred entirely within the United States. I was talking with a private investigator that specialized in social engineering. He proceeded to brag and "confess" about a project he worked on circa 2005. According to him, a large-chain paint company had decided they wanted to open an outlet in a city in the Midwest in the U.S. There was an especially successful small paint store in the city so the investigator was tasked with finding out about their business operations. After trying several low-keyed techniques, the investigator launched a scheme to try and gather the needed information. He contacted the store owner and claimed to be a professor at the local university's business administration college. He told the owner, playing to his ego, that he had heard great things about his business and wondered if he could have a couple students join him and interview the owner for a case study. The owner agreed. The investigator then went to the college and hired two students, a male and female, who were known to be involved in the university theater as actors in plays. He paid them to play the role of business majors and gave them some questions and

[4] Peter Schweizer, *Friendly Spies: How America's Allies Are Using Economic Espionage to Steal Our Secrets*, Atlantic Monthly Press, 1993, pp. 186-187.

interrogatories that he needed answers to. The three showed up at the store and met with the owner. Playing on his ego, the individuals were able to get business plans, pricing data, and cost data that never should have been given to anyone. The "professor" commented on how this demonstrated that using good basic business principles could make a business successful. He even got some university letterhead and sent a letter to the store owner thanking him and praising him for supporting the learning objectives of the college of business at the university. According to the investigator, up until he went out of business when the new chain moved into the community and undercut his pricing and sales strategy, the owner had the bogus letter from the university framed and on the wall in his office. He had never bothered to check and see if the name provided for the professor and students was even valid or if the visit to his store was university sanctioned. Of course, it was not and sadly it contributed to his business demise. An otherwise good businessman, unaware of the threats he faced even as a small business, became the victim of a professional business spy and a fake "tour" of his business.

During other tours, we have often seen individuals breaking away to go to the restroom, etc., and later found them wandering around unsupervised after claiming they got lost and could not find the tour group.

All of these examples prove that would be unwise for any company that has sensitive processes underway or sensitive information available in a facility to give tours of their facilities. Tours can make a business vulnerable.

Vulnerabilities Identified

As in the examples discussed in other chapters, the employees in the examples of physical theft and appropriation were not prepared for the espionage threats they encountered. There was no formal education and awareness program to explain threats and the *modus operandi* (including office/home break-ins and trash covers) to watch for inside the United States, Europe, Asia, and Latin America.

Additionally:
- There was no formal program for reporting possible business espionage.
- Those responsible for security often did not see the linkage between information of value to competitors and state-sponsored spies and poor physical security that allowed the information (through its hosts) to be stolen.

- Very few sensitive documents or materials were locked up and protected. For example, there was no secondary barrier in the law firm, individual offices were not locked, computers were not secured, and a binder with recipes valued at more than US$30 million was just laying out where a spy in a lab coat could snatch it. The same was true of the customer list left lying in the mailroom unattended.
- Access control and CCTV systems were not monitored live or regularly audited to determine if there were problems. Perimeter alarms and CCTV were not deployed based on the potential adverse consequences and designed to protect the most critical resources first and foremost.
- There were few programs to identify sensitive information, mark it, restrict access to it, and otherwise limit access on an absolute need-to-know basis.
- Few companies do a good job of ensuring paper or documents that should be shredded or pulverized are actually destroyed. Even if the company has a robust and effective program in the office, few are prepared for the "home office" threats too.
- Most computers were not encrypted or otherwise protected in case they were stolen.
- There was a limited security approach and little or no education and awareness training on the threats.
- There was a lack of due diligence/background investigations on employees, contractors, and business partners.
- There was no due diligence or advanced screening of individuals participating in tours/visits of facilities where there was the potential of sensitive information being compromised.

Summary

While the *modus operandi* of simply breaking into a location to copy or steal business secrets can be countered with good physical security measures employed to protect from the threats of theft, robbery, or workplace violence, it is important to understand that this is a specific method regularly used by business spies. When something is missing and there appears to be no reason why that particular item was taken instead of a similar item left untouched nearby, or there is sensitive data involved, it is time to recognize that this could mean this was a case involving business espionage. While sometimes a theft is about the actual device, many times it is about the information it stores.

As we have seen, the loss of sensitive information does not even have to involve a physical "break-in." There may be other ways a spy can get access to a facility, such as by posing as a job applicant or visitor on a tour. If employees are not trained and rules enforced to prevent sensitive information from being thrown into the trash, information can be recovered from trash bins.

It is important for employees to know why there are access control measures in place and the importance of secondary barriers. Staff members who likely deal with outsiders should be trained and alert to social engineering techniques. All sensitive material and information should be identified, marked, and secured. Security systems should be designed to allow early detection of threats and specific protection of critical information/resources.

6

FACING ESPIONAGE WHILE TRAVELING

Abstract

This chapter includes information on how vulnerable travelers and expatriates are while doing business in foreign countries. Unfortunately, in spite of high threats by state-sponsored intelligence agencies, business competitors and professional spies, many business travelers do not get education and awareness training on the threats. Instead travel security education and awareness continues to focus on physical threats from terrorism, criminal groups, unrest, weather and health issues. In spite of potentially high adverse business impact, business espionage threats get very little attention.

Introduction

Business travelers and expatriates living in a foreign location are potentially more vulnerable to business espionage in a nation that has a culture or history of business spying. Too often the current focus of security for business travelers is only on physical security threats. Threats typically addressed in most travel security programs include terrorism, criminal activities such as robbery, kidnapping for ransom, physical dangers as a result of labor and/or political issues, medical/disease, weather, and natural disasters. There is nothing wrong with addressing these threats when traveling—they all warrant attention—but they should not

Business Espionage
© 2015 Elsevier Inc. All rights reserved.

be overemphasized at the expense of the threat of business espionage, where the adverse business impact could be severe.

It is important for expatriates and travelers to know if they might be going to a location where there are organizations that are known to target business travelers for business espionage purposes including state-sponsored intelligence agencies on behalf of the government and government-supported competitors, as well as private, professional intelligence brokers, or individual spies from their competitors.

In Chapter 3 we looked at a number of high-risk locations and examples, but there are more. The following examples took place between the mid-1990s and the present, in China, Taiwan, and Korea, as well as in Europe (France and Russia) and Latin America (Cuba, Brazil, and Venezuela) and reflect the high level of business spying that goes on when travel is involved.

Cases of Travelers Becoming Victims of Business Espionage

In addition to the examples of travelers being targeted that are covered in other chapters, the following are examples of how travelers can be extremely vulnerable to business spying if they are not prepared and do not employ the appropriate countermeasures. There are a number of examples where governments and competitors have broken into hotel rooms, offices, or have otherwise electronically monitored travelers.

For example, in the 1990s when Russia was transitioning from Communism and the Committee for State Security (KGB) was replaced by the Russian Federal Security Service or FSB, there was hope that the electronic monitoring that took place with visitors to the Soviet Union would no longer happen. Unfortunately, the monitoring is still widely occurring in Russia.

During the transition period, a couple, both of whom were mid-level employees of a company, went to a tourist hotel in Russia. Interestingly, the company they worked for required a pre-travel briefing because the company did some defense-related work. The couple was pre-briefed by corporate security and was told that their room would probably have audio and/or video monitoring. The couple was asked to come back for a debriefing by corporate security after they returned from travel to Russia. When the couple was being debriefed by corporate security they described a situation in Moscow where they were having trouble sleeping because of the suspected monitoring. While they were told to do nothing to remove suspected devices, the couple admitted that they had not followed that advice. The husband said that he saw a "lump" under the carpet. The carpet was not fastened down and was only rolled over the floor and there was a small bump in the carpet at about the center of the room. He said he rolled the carpet back and saw what he thought was a "pressure plate." The couple described the "pressure plate" as a metal circular disk, fastened down by a series of bolts around the edge of the disk. The man said he was fairly certain that when you entered the room and stepped upon the carpet, it pressed down on the "plate" and activated the monitoring equipment. He therefore removed the nuts/bolts and lifted the pressure plate off and then rolled the carpet back. No longer being monitored, in their minds, the couple said they had a good night's sleep. The next morning, they said, as they walked through the lobby, hotel staff came up to them and asked if they were in room 812. The couple said they smiled and acknowledged that that was indeed their room. The hotel staff then asked if they were okay and everything was all right. Again, the couple smiled (knowingly) and said they were fine. The hotel staff revealed they were happy to hear that and shared that sometime during the night, the light fixture mounted on the ceiling of room 712 had fallen on the occupants of that room right below this couple's room. While this is humorous, in a sense, it does illustrate that travel security briefings need to be thorough and travelers should not take countermeasures into their own hands, beyond what actions they take to limit disclosures while traveling and in a hotel room or other venue.

In the mid-1990s, the regional security officer (RSO) of a government diplomatic staff was staying in a hotel in Taipei, Taiwan while working with companies on business deals in Taiwan. He left his room in a hurry for a meeting and jumped into a government vehicle. Just as they were pulling out of the hotel, the individual realized he had accidently left his expensive Mont Blanc pen lying on the bedside stand in his hotel room. He asked the driver to go back to the hotel and jumped out of the vehicle outside of the hotel compound and ran inside. Since he was in a hurry, he ran up the stairwell to the fourth floor, where his room was located, instead of taking the elevator. When he entered his room he found six people looking through his personal stuff and removing a disc from a recording device in the ceiling, which was co-located with the smoke detector. Needless to say, they were surprised to see the occupant had returned and claimed they were hotel maintenance, but the RSO, being knowledgeable of espionage, saw what they were doing and the equipment they had. He subsequently had other business people from his country advise him of similar occurrences in Taiwan and China.

In another incident that took place in the late 1990s, a group of U.S. businesspeople traveled to Seoul, South Korea, where they had made reservations in a large chain hotel in Seoul. The purpose of the visit was to address legal action that was being taken against a Korean conglomerate group. The company arranged to have all of their staff housed on the same floor and was able to obtain a conference room on the same floor, which was used as the "legal command center." At night, after working all day, the team would lock the conference room and get together for dinner and drinks. After two different days where it appeared that some documents had been moved, the team decided to call for a Technical Surveillance Countermeasures (TSCM) survey. During the survey, TSCM personnel detected microphones in the rooms of some of the team members. Hidden cameras were also installed in the legal command center. Upon review, the next day, the recordings inside the command center disclosed that about 2 a.m. what appeared to be members of the hotel security team entered the command center with a key and began going through documents and taking pictures. The question was why was the hotel security doing this? It was subsequently determined that the Korean group the foreign company was taking legal action against also owned this hotel chain in Korea. It was no surprise then that the hotel staff was providing intelligence on the legal planning. The better question was why someone would select to stay in a hotel owned by a group they were taking legal action against. The answer, of course, was no one checked on who owned the hotel.

Several years ago, a U.S. company was concerned about repeated instances where sensitive business information was apparently being lost by their business travelers while in hotels in China. The company went so far as to set up hidden cameras and microphones in the rooms of several mid-level executives traveling in China. They wanted to know if the monitoring extended to mid-level employees. According to the company, shortly after the employees left, individuals entered the rooms and began to systematically search the room and go through papers left behind. At one point, one of the individuals conducting the search found one of the hidden cameras. When he brought it to the apparent team leader, the leader openly expressed concern that another Chinese intelligence service was already targeting the visitors. He told his team to leave the hidden camera and get out of the room so as not to disrupt the organization's spying mission.

In 2008, three U.S.-based R & D employees traveled to Wuhan, China, and brought their laptop computers with them, which contained extensive sensitive R & D-related information. After working for several days in Wuhan, some staff in the office invited the three out for dinner and drinks. Their Chinese hosts within the company convinced the employees to lock their laptops in one of the manager's offices; they were told they could return to the office after the evening's festivities were over to get them and return to their hotel. They had a good evening of eating and fellowship, but when two of the group said they were tired and ready to return to their hotel, the Chinese hosts insisted everyone have at least one more drink. The drinks dragged on, but finally, about 11 p.m., they returned to the office. As the group entered the office and passed by a glass door that opened into the emergency fire exit stairwell, everyone noticed that the door was broken and glass was scattered in the stairwell. As they slowly entered the office area, someone noticed the office door where the laptops had been stored, had also been broken into and, when they entered, all three laptops were missing. The employees summoned building security, which, in turn, called the police. Efforts to get with building security to view the CCTV coverage in the stairwell were unsuccessful because building security claimed the CCTV system just happened to not be working on the floor where the incident took place. According to building security the CCTV cameras had supposedly failed to work that night and repairs were not completed until the next day. The CCTV camera in the elevator lobby was working but a review only showed the three visiting persons and their hosts. It appeared that someone took stairs up to the floor and entered the stairwell from another floor. A review of CCTV cameras inside the elevators did show one suspicious individual but he was wearing dark glasses and a hat that hid most of his features from the single fixed camera in the elevator. He got off on the floor just below the office area that was broken into. A review of crime-scene photographs and investigation determined that the glass in the stairwell door, which should have been on the inside of the office area if someone had broken into the office area, was almost exclusively on the outside of the door, which indicated the door was broken outward from someone on the inside. If the thief or thieves were already on the inside there would be no reason to break the glass (the door had an emergency push bar for exit) except if the broken door and glass was designed to mislead or misrepresent what happened. Given that the only items taken (and there were at least 20-30 other laptops, mobile telephones, and even cash lying on or inside desks that were not touched) were the three laptops from the visiting R & D staff and the only break-in occurred in the interior office where the three laptops were kept, it was apparent the theft had occurred because of inside knowledge. About three weeks later, after an intensive internal investigation by the company, the Wuhan police suddenly reported they had found the thief and recovered the laptops. The thief was allegedly an "itinerant" who was not authorized to be in Wuhan. The police maintained he had kept the three laptops with him until they unexplainably caught him. When the laptops were returned to the United States, a forensic study of the computers showed that all the data on all three computers had been downloaded.

Business travelers should also know that waiters/waitresses can be required to elicit information and serve as collectors in the People's Republic of China. Women also work bars and clubs in China, gathering information. In 2011, the Japanese media interviewed an attractive young Chinese woman who acknowledged that she had been recruited by Chinese military intelligence and was reporting information. Her job was to work the bars in Beijing where foreigners would go. The young lady said she was told to keep talking to foreigners and try and find those who could provide information of value. She said she was never specifically instructed to obtain specific documents or information, but was asked to at least find out details about plans for business, even future business trips or information about the target's colleagues. For this information, the young lady received a free apartment in Beijing and a bonus of several thousand Chinese Yuan every time she succeeded in obtaining information.[1]

It is worth knowing that travelers are subject to monitoring, as we have noted above and in other chapters, in places such as Korea, Taiwan, China, and Russia. It is also well known, within counterintelligence circles, that the French have a special unit, known when I was in the counterintelligence business as "Unit Sept," or Unit 7. One of the former Unit 7 team members told me that on average they went through more than eight hotel rooms a day, examining documents, computers, etc. It was widely reported in the news media that the unit was also responsible for putting video cameras and microphones into first-class seats of Air France flights to read documents/computer screens and listen to business people who worked or talked on the plane. The former head of the French General Directorate of External Security (DGSE), Pierre Marion, acknowledged the unit's activities during an interview according to the *Philadelphia Inquirer*.[2]

It is also well known that hotel staff will cooperate with the national intelligence services when those agencies want to get into rooms of business travelers. French, Korean, Chinese, and Taiwanese hotel staff have all reported that they had no choice but to let government services into specified rooms. I spoke with the manager of a western hotel chain in China, for example, and he reported that they had to open up rooms and even room safes for government security agencies. The manager was an ethnic

---

[1] Kenji Minemura, "Chinese Military Used Wide Network of Female Spies," *Asahi Weekly*, November 9, 2011.
[2] Frank Greve, "In World Espionage, France Emerges as Key U.S. Adversary," *Philadelphia Inquirer*, October 24, 1992, http://www.articles.philly.com/1992-10-28/news/25999062_1_aerospace-industry-air france-dgse

Chinese-American citizen but he said the Chinese security agency made it clear that there would be big problems with regulatory agencies if China did not cooperate. Another travel agency manager, who specialized in trips to Latin America, said he had multiple examples of electronic monitoring of hotel rooms, and intelligence service entry into rooms in both Cuba and in Venezuela. This conversation also occurred with a Tampa-based travel agent who had taken tour groups into both Cuba and Venezuela. In both countries, individuals had returned to their rooms to find individuals going through their property or found items had been moved, including papers/documents kept inside of the hotel safe. As the U.S. government contemplates opening up travel and business with Cuba, it will be important for travelers and business people going to Cuba to understand the intelligence threat there and prepare accordingly. For example, they should know that their rooms are monitored by at least audio and possibly video. Hotel, restaurant, bar and tourist staff will report on their activities and telephone/computer communications are subject to monitoring. In fact, the use of travel agencies to help in spying on travelers to Cuba goes back to reports published in the *Miami Herald* in 1999.[3]

Vulnerabilities Identified

These examples drive home the point that many employees traveling are not adequately prepared for the threats they face. There are few travel security programs that address business-spying threats.

All too frequently traveling employees do not receive training that would instruct them to:

- Not discuss sensitive information in an individual room or meeting room, especially if there has been no TSCM or protection implemented.
- Not leave any sensitive documents or computers in a hotel room, office, or meeting room; instead, they should be told to keep them on their person at all times or not bring them at all to a high-threat country.
- Not use the hotel safe to store any sensitive business information.
- Not work on sensitive documents while on an aircraft, in a business lounge, hotel room, etc.
- Be careful when using a computer in a hotel or visiting office area.

---

[3] Martin Arostegui, "Spy Ring for Cuba Uncovered," *Miami Herald*, January 19, 1999, http://www.latinamericanstudies.org/espionage/uncovered.html

- Conduct TSCM sweeps, or at least expert visual inspections, prior to using an area and keep it secured throughout the time of the visit.
- Do not discuss sensitive information in restaurants, bars and clubs and do not discuss any sensitive business information with staff of hotels, bars, restaurants, etc. at any time but especially when traveling or near your office.

Every company should have a business espionage travel security education and awareness program that includes training on how to protect sensitive information while traveling. Companies should also interview and debrief all travelers when they return from a trip to see if there have been any business-spying attempts. This latter step is needed to drive home the importance the company places on protecting sensitive information from business espionage.

Conclusion

Most travel security news summaries and many company programs focus on protecting company travelers from physical security threats but almost none of these address one of the most severe travel threats, one that could cause a major adverse business impact—the threat of business espionage. As a result of this lack of training and *laissez faire* attitude, too often business travelers are "easy pickings" for many business spies. While the possibility of violence a traveler might face is certainly a concern, it is equally important to consider the business impact/consequences that business espionage could pose. Interestingly enough, some of the threats with the highest adverse business impact/consequence are low on the violence spectrum (Figure 6.1) and many companies have failed to understand that difference.

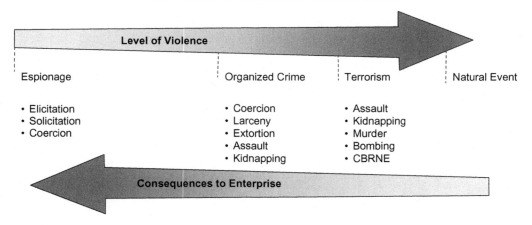

Figure 6.1 Some threats of espionage, while low on the violence spectrum, have a high business impact.

I have reviewed the top 10 travel security daily reports and threat ratings (unfortunately many also incorrectly use the term "risk" rating), and none of them consistently address business espionage in the various countries covered in their reports. Since this is one of the main tools used for traveler security education, this leaves a major gap (vulnerability) in travel security education. While the majority of U.S.-headquartered multinational companies involved in the U.S. State Department's Overseas Security Advisory Council (OSAC) said they had travel controls in place for countries known to have a serious criminal or terrorist threat, only a handful (most of those because of classified government contracts) had similar travel restrictions for travel to countries known to pose a high threat for business espionage. This needs to change!

Note that the adverse business impact to an enterprise is often higher for less violent threats such as espionage than for more violent threats such as terrorism, assault, kidnapping, murder, etc. In spite of this, many enterprises continue to focus their travel security and overall security programs on the levels of violence they expect and ignore the high-consequence business espionage threats.

Interestingly enough, two of the 11 Russians sleeper agents arrested and charged with espionage against the United States in 2010 were involved in the travel agent business.[4] It is a good way to determine who to target (name, business, etc.) and to get them in the desired room that has the needed cameras and microphones installed.

As if that is not enough, a 2014 report by Kaspersky Lab revealed that hackers are able to compromise luxury hotel Wi-Fi networks and traveling business executives into downloading malicious software that can result in their business information being accessed remotely. The software from hotels has been labeled "Darkhotel" espionage and about 90 percent of the known infections appear to be occurring in Japan, Taiwan, China, Russia and South Korea but the focus is clearly executives doing business and investment in the Asia-Pacific or European regions.[5] Once again, traveling and using hotel networks for business communications is fraught with business espionage vulnerabilities.

[4] Sarah DiLorenzo, "The Russian Spies Who Loved U.S.," *Huffington Post*, May 14, 2013, http://www.huffingtonpost.com/2013/05/14/russian-spies-us-espionage_n_3274988.html
[5] "Hackers Target CEOs in 'Darkhotel' Scheme," The China Post, November 12, 2014, page 6.

7

INSIDER THREAT

CHAPTER OUTLINE
Introduction 85
Cases of Insider Espionage 87
Vulnerabilities Identified 96
Summary 97

Abstract

This chapter includes information on one of the most significant and common threats – the insider. It discusses a number of infamous insider spies and many insider spy incidents that have never been publically disclosed. Examples cover the full spectrum of large, high tech and small or low tech firms. Some insider spies are high level employees but many are also secretaries and administrative staff. Insider spies are not just employees but also include contractors including cleaning staff, security staff, etc.

Introduction

Insider threat is one of the most common and potentially serious threats of business espionage. In the espionage world there are numerous examples of governments and competitors placing spies within targeted locations. This is often called "planting" a spy. Another option is to get someone who already has legitimate access to sensitive information to provide it. This can be what is called an "in-place" recruitment, and this kind of recruitment provides regular inside information to an espionage agent. Another option that is frequently used is to offer an individual a higher-paying position in a competitive firm and have the individual bring sensitive information with them. This is often done by recruitment firms that "recruit away" targeted talent. Of all of the options, the preferred approach is to recruit but then keep

Business Espionage
© 2015 Elsevier Inc. All rights reserved.

an insider working inside of the company because the competitor then has continual access to the latest information.

Businesses are at risk for insider threats from both state-sponsored intelligence agencies working on behalf of a government and/or government-supported competitors (state-owned companies). Competitors themselves can also use an insider, sometimes directly and sometimes using a third-party agency that serves as the "handler" for the spy. These parties use insiders to gather information of all kinds that could potentially have business value, including data on pricing, sales strategies, personal data, computer data, business documents, finance documents, bidding, and pricing. The value of an insider is that you not only have documents and materials, you may also have insight into thought processes and plans that have not been written down.

One technique that can be used is called the "honey pot" or "honey trap" method where the initial angle is romantic and/or sexual. If the individual is truly attached to the person who seduces them, information can be obtained over a long period. The spy may trust his or her lover enough to reveal secrets, or may even change their loyalty and allegiance because of their emotional attachment, but even if the spy does not deliberately give information to their lover, the lover may accidentally be given opportunities to obtain it themselves. A long-term relationship is not necessarily the goal, but a long-term relationship does mean a continued source of information. This technique can be used to blackmail anyone who later regrets their actions and tries to change course. Incriminating photo/videos or recordings can be an effective tool of coercion, for example.

An infamous example of this was the Taiwanese general who was allegedly seduced by a Chinese female while the general served as an attaché in Thailand. The general initially gave in and provided information to his "lover," but later there was an allegation of blackmail where the general allegedly received up to US$1 million for information he provided. As is often the case, his motivations were complex, but the bottom line is that he was an "insider" with legitimate access to much of what he provided to Chinese intelligence services.[1]

Here are some other examples of the alleged use of this technique:

- Clayton J. Lonetree, an embassy guard in Moscow, was entrapped by a female Soviet officer in 1987. He was then blackmailed into handing over documents when he was assigned to Vienna.
- Roy Rhodes, a U.S. Army Non-Commissioned Officer serving at the U.S. embassy in Moscow, had a one-night stand (or was

---

[1] "Taiwan, China in Talks Over Spy Swap," *South China Morning Post*, December 16, 2013.

made to believe he had) with a Soviet agent while drunk. He was later told the agent was pregnant, and that unless he cooperated with the Soviet authorities, this would be revealed to his wife.

- Irvin Scarbeck, a U.S. diplomat, was entrapped by a female Polish officer in 1961 and photographed in a compromising position. He was blackmailed into providing secrets.
- Sharon Scranage, a CIA employee described by one source as a "shy, naive, country girl," was allegedly seduced by Ghanaian intelligence agent Michael Soussoudis. She gave him information on CIA operations in Ghana, which was later shared with Soviet-bloc countries.
- James J. Smith and William Cleveland, two FBI officers, are alleged to have been seduced by Katrina Leung in order to obtain information.
- Mordechai Vanunu, who had disclosed Israeli nuclear secrets, began an affair with an American Mossad agent, Cheryl Bentov, operating under the name "Cindy" and masquerading as an American tourist, on September 30, 1986. She persuaded him to fly to Rome, Italy with her on a holiday. Once in Rome, Mossad agents drugged him and smuggled him to Israel on a freighter.
- John Vassall, a British civil servant who was guided by the KGB into having sex with multiple male partners while drunk. The KGB then used photographs of this to blackmail Vassall into providing them with secret information.[2]

Insider threat is one of the most significant threats but many companies do not address it because they think it would imply a lack of trust of all employees or those that have legitimate access to sensitive information. Companies prefer to develop programs that are designed exclusively for external threats but are reluctant to address the all too common insider threat. Given the frequency of insider recruitments it is important for companies to stop their "head in the sand" approach to this threat and realistically consider how this issue should be addressed.

The examples that follow took place from the mid-1990s to the present in China, Taiwan, Japan, Korea, and India and are only a few of the many examples of the insidious insider problem.

Cases of Insider Espionage

In the mid-1990s, an international security firm was targeted by competition in South Korea. The South Korean competitor had an older Korean woman call the international firm's younger

---

[2] Jack King, author, spywriter.com/robots/honeypot.html.

secretary and try and arrange a meeting at a nearby coffee shop. The excuse was that the older secretary wanted to learn more about how to get a job with a foreign company. The secretary was suspicious and reported this unusual call to her supervisor. She was instructed to agree to a meeting when the older woman called again. Within a day, the call came and plain clothes security personnel were deployed to the coffee shop where they observed, photographed, and recorded the older woman as she tried to persuade the young secretary to provide pricing and customer data to the South Korean competitor. The spy was given a special cell telephone that could be used to contact her handling agent as well as some money. She was promised more money and even a possible job if she continued to spy on the international company. The older woman noted that the international company would not give her a true opportunity for promotion and she felt she could help South Korean companies be competitive and make some additional money at the same time. When the handling agent was confronted by security staff, she admitted that she worked for a competitor and was trying to get someone who had access to pricing, customer lists, and methodologies that could be used to help the company get some of the business that was going to the international competitor.

In the late 1990s, a young, attractive woman in Taipei, Taiwan was approached by an older man who was a senior executive for a Japanese firm operating in Taiwan. She worked for a real-estate company that had the Japanese company as a client. Part of their service included providing office space and housing for Japanese expatriates in Taiwan. During the course of a conversation, the Japanese executive asked the Taiwanese female about her long-term life and career objectives. The young woman shared that she was taking college courses at night in an effort to enhance her skills in administrative areas. The Japanese executive took an immediate interest and began wining and dining the young lady. She initially thought it might be a romantic interest; however, it became clear that he had a genuine interest in her learning and progressing. When she had difficulties with finances for tuition and needed a computer in order to stay ahead, the Japanese executive jumped in to help. He pushed the young woman to work hard and complete her classes. When she completed her studies, he took her on a trip to Singapore where they flew first class and stayed (in separate rooms) in a five-star hotel. At a dinner before they returned to Taipei, the Japanese executive told the young woman that he wanted her to apply for an opening as an executive secretary in the front office of a competing Taiwanese firm. He assured the young lady that with her language skills, her computer and administrative skills, and her good looks she would get the job. He then told her she should pay him back for his generosity by providing information on the business. After attending one of my presentations on business espionage, the young woman came up to talk. This had just happened and she wanted to know whether if she provided information if she would end up in trouble or in jail. I told her that while it was doubtful that providing information was technically illegal it was definitely not ethical. She agreed and ultimately declined to seek the position.

In 2005, a U.S. high-tech manufacturing company contacted me and asked if I could do a detailed background investigation on an individual the company had hired from China. I confirmed that the individual had been hired and had worked at the company's headquarters for almost 6 months. The corporate security director reported that the individual supposedly had a degree in the field he was working in but his co-workers were questioning his skills. I asked if they had conducted a pre-employment background investigation and the security director said they had not because the individual lived and had gone to college in the People's Republic of China. After conducting a background check it was apparent that the college the individual allegedly attended was, in fact, well known for educating personnel for a Chinese intelligence service. This information was verbally provided to the corporate security director who then exclaimed, "Aha! So that's why the FBI was here asking about him!" That was the extent of my involvement in this matter so I do not know what happened next. However, I did see the security director later and he thanked me for the information and voluntarily added that the information was of great value since the individual would have otherwise had access to some very sensitive inside information. I asked him why the company had not asked us to do a pre-employment background investigation prior to hiring the individual and he said that the company's human resources department had told him that it would be expensive and unnecessary, in their opinion, to do checks in China but now all had learned their lesson.

In 2007, a U.S. high-tech firm asked me to conduct an investigation on an engineer who had worked in their research and development office for 5 years and had suddenly resigned—supposedly, he said, to go back to Taiwan and be with his family. We were able to locate the individual in Taipei and put him under surveillance to see what he was doing. On the second day of surveillance, the individual was followed to the offices of a high-tech competitor company in the Hsinchu Science and Industry Park on the outskirts of Taipei. Further inquiries at the competing firm confirmed that the former employee was now the head of the competitor's research and development department and was being paid double what he had been paid by the U.S. firm. Subsequently it became apparent to the American company that their Taiwan competitor had benefited from the information the former engineer had learned while working for them. What caused exceptional concern was that the engineer had just been promoted and given a bonus and an increase in salary after being named an outstanding engineer in the company's research and development division. Company executives were shocked when, in spite of this, the individual announced he was leaving.

One of the most recent incidents I have seen—which is very similar to the senior executive at General Motors who was recruited in the 1990s by the competitor Volkswagen and who literally took crates of material with him—involved a senior executive at Harsco Corporation in Harrisburg, Pennsylvania in the U.S. Harsco Corporation filed suit against one of its former top executives in federal court, accusing him of corporate espionage for allegedly passing confidential company information to a competitor. According to court documents, Clyde Kirkwood essentially acted as a mole. Kirkwood abruptly quit his post as commercial vice president for Harsco's Metals & Minerals Division in early June, 3 months after he secretly agreed to take an executive job with the Michigan-based Edw. C. Levy Co., according to the Harsco lawsuit. Harsco claims that, starting early that year, Kirkwood not only passed confidential Harsco information to Levy, including data on top-level corporate decisions, he also intervened to try to steer Harsco away from international projects that would have been in competition with Levy. Harsco's lawyers refer to the alleged espionage as "shocking," especially since it involved an ex-employee who worked for Harsco for 23 years, had risen steadily through the corporate ranks, and was trusted implicitly. They claim that Kirkwood, a citizen of the United Kingdom, accepted his final promotion from Harsco in April, a month after he had secretly accepted a $420,000-a-year vice president job with Levy. They alleged that Kirkwood also passed confidential corporate information to an industry consultant, Geoffrey Butler, a former Harsco president who retired 4 years previously (Butler is not a defendant in the suit). Harsco's suit is understandable as the firm has more than 12,000 employees and provides logistical and environmental support and engineering services to industries worldwide. Kirkwood was considered one of the company's top 100 employees, the Harsco suit states, and contends that he began secretly soliciting employment with Levy in January, using his wife's email. Soon after, he began passing information to Levy, including information regarding a potential Harsco project involving a steel mill in Israel, the suit states. Harsco claims Kirkwood actively tried to deter it from considering that project. He also allegedly passed Levy inside information on a possible Harsco project with a company in India, and on projects in Brazil and Oman, Harsco alleges. By remaining with Harsco after he supposedly accepted the Levy job, "Kirkwood continued to benefit from very high-level access to Harsco's most confidential business and proprietary information, including trade secrets," the suit states.[3]

It never ceases to amaze me how many times companies even inadvertently pay for being spied on. In Chapter 3, I shared the story of electronic eavesdropping devices purchased on a company credit card by employees before they left the company and planted the devices. In 2014, an automotive parts manufacturing company operating in Canada was developing some new, modified, and updated automotive equipment. One of their employees was able to take some prototypes and mail them, through the company mail room and mail service, to one of their peripheral business partners. When the devices were determined to be missing an investigation was launched and the individual who took them claimed that he accidently and inadvertently mailed them to the business partner. While it seemed to be an innocent mistake, when efforts were made to get the prototypes back, the partner failed to cooperate. Ultimately it was determined that they were closely linked to a competitor who was now releasing a similar device. The individual who supposedly "accidently" mailed them suddenly resigned and joined the competing firm and the victim company realized they had been victims of insider business spying.

Insiders are not always direct employees. They are sometimes contractors who have legitimate access to facilities. A company in Mexico called me in 2012 and reported that they had an unusual incident where an individual working as a contract cleaner had been spotted by one of their engineers. Their engineer realized that this suspicious-acting cleaner was a classmate from the university where they both had studied engineering. He was shocked to see this well-educated individual working as a contract cleaner, and when he advised security, they attempted to confront the individual. He tried to run away but was detained. When questioned, he admitted that he had been sent by his company, a

[3]Matt Miller, "Corporate Espionage? Harsco Sues Ex-Exec It Claims Passed Secrets to Competitor; Consultant, " *Harrisburg Patriot-News*, July 2, 2014, http://www.pennlive.com/midstate/index.ssf/2014/07/corporate_espionage_harsco_sue.html

competing company, to try and learn about their processes. They had determined that being a cleaner he would not be suspected and would have unrestricted access to the areas he needed to see. He even admitted to having brought concealed cameras into the facility and had taken photos of their processes.

In another example (circa 2005) a U.S. company found it necessary to lay off employees at one of its China offices and at its Hong Kong office. Obviously, management wanted to keep these plans confidential until the details were worked out and they were ready to discuss them with employees. However, management was surprised when they were suddenly confronted by angry workers who had learned of the planned move prior to its announcement. It seems an IT employee in the Hong Kong office, who was among those who were going to be laid off, had been reading confidential e-mails between the company's general manager in Hong Kong and the corporate headquarters in the U.S. The employee shared all the information with other employees and, of course, the news spread quickly and caused problems with sabotage, threats to management, and loss of equipment and information.

In 2010, I was conducting a risk assessment for a high-tech multinational company operating in New Delhi, India. During the course of conducting the assessment I went to the basement to check on what might have been in the regular trash being removed by the cleaning crew. As I entered the dock area where the trash was being consolidated I found that two cleaning company employees were going through the trash and pulling out documents and laying them out on the dock. When they saw me they tried to cover up the documents with plastic garbage bags but I walked around and pulled back the garbage bags and found a number of company documents, including some that had proprietary and confidential markings. The cleaning crew claimed they sorted through the trash in order to get paid extra for recycling paper but a lot of other paper documents were still in the trash and the ones that had been pulled out and laid out on the dock were those that contained sensitive information—information that never should have been in the regular trash according to the company's policy on information protection (the company used a document destruction company and also had a number of shredders placed around their offices).

Just after an incident detailed elsewhere in this book, where employees bought and planted listening devices before they resigned and left Hong Kong, another company called and asked us to do a TSCM survey and risk assessment, since it seemed to them that some of their employees knew certain sensitive information that had been kept secret. During discussions the employees would occasionally mention things that had only been discussed behind closed doors, which puzzled company leadership. A thorough TSCM assessment was done during off-hours and no active covert listening devices were found. During the assessment, however, it was noted that the company had an extensive speaker phone system installed within their conference room and even in the general manager's office. Company leadership agreed to hold a telephonic conference with corporate headquarters in the U.S. and have us do some discreet monitoring from one of the senior manager's offices during work hours. The veteran TSCM auditor began to see problems immediately, and we were able to trace the electronic monitoring to an employee's cubicle where we found an employee listening to the meeting. He had left a portable microphone that was used for presentations in the room and he had turned it on so he could listen using a headset. He later acknowledged that he had shared the information with several other colleagues who were worried about downsizing in the Hong Kong office and were lining up jobs with competitors based on this information.

A hospital in the United States called me, in 2003, and asked for a thorough assessment and TSCM survey because some patients had complained that they had received calls from someone who obviously had inside medical information about some personally sensitive medical treatment they had received. Initially it was thought the information might have come from administrative staff, nurses or others that were involved in the surgeries and medical treatments. The information could have even been used for blackmailing some of the patients as it was very personal. During the course of the assessment, it was determined that the maintenance manager had some unusual software on his computer that appeared to allow him to record information. During the TSCM survey, a transmitter was found in the telephone public exchange box (PBX) that was monitoring the lines of senior hospital staff. No one suspected the maintenance manager because he would not have had access to any of the sensitive patient information but, thanks to his electronic eavesdropping device and access to the PBX closet, he also had access to the information that was compromised.

A firm called me in Hong Kong in 2000 and asked if I could find out if a current employee was being courted by his former employer to come back. The current employer was concerned that the individual would take sensitive information back to the old company, the current company's major competitor. The current employer acknowledged that when the employee had joined them, he had provided considerable sensitive information about their competitor's operations. After some calls, I was able to talk with the head of the former company. I managed to convince him that I was looking to hire this individual and I considered him, as a former boss, as a reference. The individual told me he wanted to get up and close his door, which he did, and he then told me that I would be foolish to hire the individual. He said that the individual had no ethics and had left him and took sensitive information with him to his competitor. He then added that the individual had recently called and asked about returning, promising to bring valuable information about his current company that would benefit the business. The manager said, "I was tempted but then I realized that at some point he would just do the same thing to me again." This individual, he said, "would sell his own mother." This kind of employee is out there so "buyer" beware.

In 2002, a company that specialized in manufacturing high-tech equipment told me they used some commercially available equipment in their manufacturing process but the way the equipment was used and the quality assurance techniques they had created made their product superior to their competition. They learned, however, that the maintenance people for the commercially available equipment were going to their competitors, who used some of the same basic equipment, and telling them how their company set up the commercially available equipment and details about how the specialized quality assurance measurements were conducted. After learning this, the company no longer allowed any outside service or maintenance people on their manufacturing floor. If the commercially available equipment had to be serviced, the service person was taken into and out of the manufacturing area blindfolded and in a wheel chair. Ten-foot high curtains were placed around the equipment so nothing else could be observed and security personnel monitored the activities of the maintenance person. Since instituting that policy/procedure, the company said they have not heard of any further "leaks" or compromises.

In 2001, a commercial printing firm that had operated for more than 100 years in the United States saw new competitor open up business in an adjacent city in the Midwest region of the U.S. It seems the new owner of the competitive print shop was the son of an employee of the original firm, and he got the pricing and costing details from the employee, his mother. It is believed that he also got a good list of customers. Now, years later, the start-up is still in business and the original firm has closed shop. The older firm just kept losing customers due to pricing and could not stay in business.

In 2012, an electronic game maker was working with several major international sports stars. Part of their gaming contract included some sophisticated imaging of sports stars playing their respective sports. For example, a golf star swinging his driver, a baseball star swinging his bat, and a tennis star serving. Since the sports stars' time was valuable, the company was careful with scheduling. When the stars began contacting the game maker and complaining about scheduling, it was determined that individuals pretending to be from the gaming company had persuaded the sports stars to undergo the imaging. The sports stars had incorrectly assumed they were performing and being recorded for the authorized game maker. Most likely, someone in the company, who knew about the discussions with each sports star, had used that insider information and the company name to steal valuable intellectual property from the sports stars and the game maker. In fact, at least two Asian competitors came up with games that appeared to use the same kinetic information the U.S. game maker was trying to utilize.

In 2008, in Hong Kong, an American who studied in Beijing, China, decided to stay in Beijing and work. He had learned a great deal about Chinese history and was a physical fitness buff. As a student he had frequently ridden a bicycle for cheap transportation. As an innovator, he decided to open a historic bicycle tour business in Beijing. The business took off and was very successful. In fact, it was so successful that some of employees of the company decided they could do the same thing and make more money if they opened their own competing firm. Most of the company's employees left and formed their own company, using customer lists, pricing information, and tour scripts. Within a matter of months, the American entrepreneur was forced to give up his failing business and go to work for a multinational firm. His business failed because it was the victim of business espionage.

In 2012, a large multinational aerospace company with a major manufacturing site in southern California reported some potential issues with Chinese employees that had been brought from the People's Republic of China to work at the site. Because of some of the contractual requirements, they had offices that were in a separate building but they also had access to sensitive business and manufacturing information. While the offices had CCTV monitoring, the data was only retained for investigation after something happened, and no one was actively monitoring. When one of the U.S. employees came in at night to make a call to another branch in Asia, he noticed several of the Chinese employees entering the office building across the street from the main complex. He reported this to a manager who checked the access control logs. It was determined, and confirmed by checking the CCTV records, that the Chinese employees were coming in at night on a regular basis. They were printing out data at night and were faxing and emailing it to another company in China. This had been going on for nearly 6 months and no one had detected it until it happened accidentally. Fortunately, someone finally followed up and an investigation determined a considerable amount of sensitive business data was lost to a potential competitor.

Vulnerabilities Identified

Insider threat is one of the most significant threats faced in business espionage. As I noted, companies often do not like to think about this threat because it makes them suspicious of their own employees and undermines loyalty. But the truth of the matter is that they should be a little suspicious of their own employees, because disloyal employees can do catastrophic damage. There are things a company can do to make internal spying less likely, but it's always still possible. The "ostrich syndrome" attitude (bury your head in the sand) is one of the biggest vulnerabilities a business can have when it comes to business spying. While many insider spies are working or will be working for a competitor, this doesn't mean this an external threat exclusively. If a competitor hires someone with internal access, it becomes the most dangerous threat possible: an insider and exterior threat combined.

It is also especially important to know if an individual is resigning and leaving. Such individuals may have already been taking information and it is important to check that before formal departure takes place. In the twenty-first century, this is where IT comes into the picture in for the form of a forensic examination.

Just because the individual is high level does not mean he/she cannot become a spy. There are multiple examples of this happening. Of course, it should also be clear from the examples that the insider does not have to be a high-level employee or engineer. It could be a secretary in the company. It is not who you are but what access you have.

Likewise, an "insider" may not be a direct employee. It might also be a contractor who is given access to areas such as manufacturing processes, server rooms, and executive offices. This could also be cleaning staff, security staff (see Chapter 3), contract maintenance, or others that are allowed in sensitive areas. You should think long and hard about giving contractors such as security, cleaning, and maintenance staff unsupervised access to your most sensitive areas.

It is also important to do monitoring of CCTV, access control systems, and even IT systems to look for unusual activity that warrants further investigation. These systems can offer early detection if someone does at least periodic checks to see what kind of activity is occurring. But these systems provide limited value if they are only used after a problem occurs.

Insider threats are tied to all threat vectors. Insiders can plant eavesdropping devices, they can steal information on the company IT systems, they can reveal interior strategic thinking and planning, financial data, and research/development data. Senior executives can influence decision-making within the company or office, and they can even allow individuals access that circumvents other security controls that have been put in place to protect against exterior threats.

Summary

There are many business espionage threats. While most businesses tend to focus on the outside/exterior threats, often the most damaging losses (highest consequence/business impact) occur as a result of insiders that betrayed their trust. Insiders may be employees or contractors that have authorized and legitimate access to a facility. In our examples in this and other chapters we have seen IT managers, maintenance managers, regular staff, security personnel, cleaning staff, secretaries, and R & D managers all targeted or involved in business-spying activities. They may have had different motivations but they were already inside the company or were being recruited to become an inside spy or to get inside information.

Many companies acknowledge that there is some potential business-spying threat to their sensitive business information, and some will even relent to improving physical and IT/cyber-security, conducting TSCM assessments, etc. But their approach is mainly designed to protect the company from external business-spying threats. Very few companies seem to understand that it is critically important to protect from a potential insider threat too. Realizing that one of your co-workers or employees could be a spy is just not something many companies want to deal with, but, again, this threat will not go away and it can become the most significant business espionage vulnerability you can have.

BUSINESS ESPIONAGE COUNTERMEASURES

PROTECTING YOUR MOST CRITICAL RESOURCES

Abstract

This chapter includes information on how to determine what your most critically important resources and information are. This includes Trade Secrets and any information or resources that, if compromised, could have an adverse impact on the company and its business viability. The key is to focus your business espionage countermeasures on the most critically important resources and information and not try and protect everything.

Focus on protecting the most critical information and resources

We have already indirectly stated, when we covered risk methodology in Chapter 1, that it is important to not try to protect everything all of the time. If you try to protect everything, your security can be stretched so thin that you are really not protecting much of anything well. I see this very often and it shows that the business entity is really not that committed to the specific protection of their most sensitive information. They often know they are not doing a good job of protecting their business secrets and sensitive information but they cannot bring themselves to admit it. So, instead, they turn to lots of euphemistic phrases such as "we want to have the highest levels of security for everything we do" or "our physical security and IT security staff work together very closely." While that might make them feel a bit better, if it is not completely true it can be a very dangerous mode of thinking

Business Espionage
© 2015 Elsevier Inc. All rights reserved.

because they will not be making needed improvements in their approach to security.

That is why it is important, early on in the business espionage risk assessment process, to identify and map business processes and then focus on the most important and critical information and resources—those where the loss could have the most catastrophic adverse impact on the business. The best way to start this discussion may be to simply ask key people questions such as "What do you do for a living?" "Why should someone choose our company or product over a competitor(s)?" "What makes us better than your competition?" This can help people to understand that there are things of value in the organization. Once you have achieved that basic level of understanding, it is time to determine which specific functions and types of information are the most important to your business. This will enable you to focus on protecting your most critically important resources.

Do not be side-tracked by someone saying, "There is really nothing that sensitive in our business. We use the same equipment everyone else uses and we do the same things." If that is really true, then you are right to not worry about protecting anything. You will soon be out of business as you are clearly not competitive.

Another infamous put-off I regularly hear is something like, "Our business changes so fast that by the time someone steals this information it will be outdated." While it may be true that some aspects of it will be "outdated" the spies will have profited from how you learned and where and how you progressed in earlier phases of development. Eventually they can copy the processes that helped you be so successful. Many businesses do not understand the basic tenants of intelligence, which is to gather pieces, put them together, and allow a picture to emerge.

The truth is that your company undoubtedly has some skills or techniques that work well and you need to identify and recognize those in order to protect them. You should take steps to protect what positively differentiates you from your competition. Is it quality assurance? Is it customer attention? Is it a methodology you use well? Is it the equipment you have and how you use it? The next question is, "What would the impact be on the business if the competition did this too or used this same process or technique?"

Once this truly sensitive information and these valuable resources are identified, the protective measures should be aligned so the highest standards of protection are allocated to the information with the highest potential adverse business impact. In fact, some businesses have done away with the traditional labels of "secret," "confidential," or "sensitive" (that were patterned after the military/government labels of "top secret,"

"secret," "confidential," and "for official use only") and have gone with "high business impact," "medium business impact," and "low business impact." These labels more accurately drive home the point of the classification. The high business impact information/processes/equipment should have the most layers of protection and most effective security standards and measures. Medium business impact warrants some protective standards and measures. The low business impact information, then, is the lowest priority for protective resources being expended.

One of the ways to determine the potential adverse impact is to look at the estimated value of information or other resources. This, of course, sometimes easier said than done. Physical assets are regularly assigned values, usually using a "market value," which may be determined based on replacement costs or expected revenue that will be generated. Unfortunately a lot of physical assets, and certainly most information, have value greater than just the cost of replacing the asset/information that is lost.

A laptop or a thumbdrive might have a monetary value to replace but the loss of the information stored on the device will often be far more than the value of the stolen computer or damaged file cabinet where the information is stored. This perspective requires a different way of thinking than enterprises are used to but it is an important change.

Begin an assessment by going through the information and other assets the company possesses. Identify them and make certain all of the assets and resources are listed. Then discuss the value of these assets, including the cost to research, develop and create the resource, the cost to replace the information/asset, and the value of the information to competitors or thieves. If possible, try to determine the value of lost business if a competitor is able to use this information and thus can sell the product or service at a lower price having minimal research and development or other costs invested. This is not only an important step in determining the protective measures to be employed, it is also important if there is ever a need for legal remedies.

When compiling the value of information you will have to deal with potential complacency. Staff, even leadership, of many companies are used to dealing with sensitive information during the normal course of business operations and often do not think about its value. After all, if the document jams in the printer, just pull the jammed paper out, throw it in the trash, and print another copy. The important thing is to keep going because there is likely a deadline that must be met. There is work to be done! It is difficult to get people to realize that the piece of paper or sticky note they just threw in the regular trash, which had part of the enterprise's customer base, could be of value or do damage to the enterprise if a competitor had it.

In 2014 a company reported to me that multiple external hard drives had been stolen. Company leadership was concerned about the information on one of the hard drives that contained process related information, a valid concern. However, they casually, almost nonchalantly, advised that the missing hard drive with information from the accounting division was of "little value." After probing a bit further, it was apparent that the drive with "financial information" had, among other things, a full customer list and detailed pricing information. When asked if this would not be of value to competitors, the leadership thought for a moment and then revised their assessment. They determined that the financial information was of value and actually was of major concern. This kind of questioning will probably be necessary before leadership and staff truly understand the value of what needs protected. They are not used to thinking in these terms.

Additionally, company staff members are used to dealing with day-to-day activities and, like most of us, make decisions based on a number of factors. Sometimes these day-to-day problems result in knee-jerk reactions that would not make sense months later, especially to an outsider. But that is also the value an outsider brings. For example, recently (2013) I did an assessment and found that the most sensitive information at a particular client site was undoubtedly in servers located on the top floor of a high-rise building, but there were few protective security measures in place for them. When we discussed having a security officer and monitored CCTV coverage added to enhance server room security, leadership was concerned about additional cost. When we calculated the various values of the information and compared it with the cost of additional security measures, there was no comparison as the value of the information was in the millions of dollars, while the costs measured in thousands of dollars.

Furthermore, I pointed out that there were three security officers deployed in the parking garage—one on each of the three levels in the underground parking for the building. I asked if it might not be possible to move one of those three security guard positions to the top floor where the servers were located. Management initially balked at the change because all managers wanted to make certain their reserved parking spots were protected and they were upset that, on occasion, there were people parking in them. My question was, "If someone parks in a reserved spot, what is the cost and impact on the company? On the other hand, if someone steals information from, or damages servers, what is the cost and impact on the company?" I asked if management could really say it made more sense to protect private parking spots than the server room. At that point, the senior managers all said, "When you put it like that, we need to protect those servers and it makes sense to move at least one of the guards to protect the server room." As this example illustrates, to see the forest through the trees, you have to measure all of the resources to determine which are the most critical and most valuable.

Again, start with identifying all the intellectual property and any other sensitive information. Determine all locations where that information is located and stored, which might include executive offices, finance, legal, IT, research and development, human resources, operations, and manufacturing. There may be others but as you work with each of these business entities you will find the most critical information and its location. You can then work with leadership to try and put a value on that intellectual property, sensitive information, and other assets.

Finally, in this consequence/criticality phase of the assessment it is also good to try and determine the ramifications and implications that go with the loss of any particular intellectual property and sensitive information. This is the adverse consequence or business impact aspect of the process, and can include a loss of competitive advantage and a loss of market share, or a loss of customer confidence and orders. It can also mean damage to your brand and reputation or result in loss of qualified employees and legal or regulatory problems.

One of the biggest potential adverse consequences or negative business impacts could be on the nebulous future business side of things. When you are consistently losing bids on proposals, the reason might be your ability to meet needs and your pricing, but it may also be that you are losing because competitors know your bidding process and the numbers you are submitting. It is not hard to undercut you when armed with that information.

The French were quite good at seeing the positive economic impact of their business espionage operations. Pierre Marion boasts that during his tenure as the head of France's external spy agency, France won a $2 billion airplane deal with India thanks to the business-espionage-derived information that was gathered by French intelligence. The late French spy chief Count de Marenches typified the French view when he wrote in his memoirs that economic espionage is "very profitable. . . . In any intelligence service worthy of the name you would easily come across cases where the whole year's budget has been paid for in full by a single operation."[1]

---

[1] Peter Schweizer, "Growth of Economic Espionage: America is Target Number One," *Foreign Affairs* Magazine, January/February 1996.

It is wise to look at the potential adverse consequences in a similar manner. If the French won a US$2 billion airplane deal due to business spying, an American company lost a potential US$2 billion airplane deal due to business espionage. That's a major adverse impact. If spies are paying for themselves in a business sense and are justifying their annual budgets based on this kind of business gain, the counterespionage operations can have the same impact. If a counterespionage element of a business is able to keep the company's business secrets protected and enable the company to successfully make competitive bids and sell new, innovative state-of-the-market equipment and services, it has easily paid for itself.

It is also of value to determine if a potential business partner shares your concerns about integrity and protecting intellectual property. I was impressed with a U.S. firm who asked me to come along with their legal and security staff as they checked out a potential manufacturing partner in Taiwan in 1996. The company, which manufactured a specialized type of sports equipment, went to the Hsinchu Industrial Park in Taiwan to check out a company that manufactured the same type of sports equipment for use within that country. After viewing their manufacturing facility, the U.S. company representatives sat down, in a conference room, with the Taiwan manufacturing firm's leadership. The lead attorney for the U.S. company advised that they would expect a separate and closed off manufacturing line. The Taiwan company leadership responded, "no problem." Then the legal team from the U.S. pointed out that the company had never manufactured any of its products outside of the U.S. and made the comment, "All of our products must say, "made in the USA." At that point the Taiwan company chairman said, "No problem. We can put 'made in the USA' on what we manufacture." At that point the leader of the due diligence team said he had heard all he needed to hear and asked his team to gather up their things and head to their vehicles. The Taiwan manufacturing chief seemed puzzled. As the Americans walked out the door he kept asking his staff, "What did I say that was bad. I agreed to do anything they wanted?" Sometimes it is good to see where a company and its leadership draw the line and where their levels of business integrity are before becoming a partner with them and sharing valuable intellectual property.

One other concern is worth mentioning here. You should work legal professionals to determine if any of the sensitive information qualifies as a legal "trade secret." The precise language defining a trade secret varies from jurisdiction to jurisdiction, but there are generally three factors common to all information that qualifies as a trade secret:

- It is not generally known to the public;
- It confers some sort of economic benefit to its holder (where this benefit must derive *specifically* from its not being publicly known, not just from the value of the information itself);
- Has the owning entity made "reasonable" efforts to protect it from compromise?

Interestingly, these three aspects are also incorporated in Article 39 of the TRIPS Agreement.[2] What it means to an enterprise is that they must take specific steps to establish that this sensitive information (trade secret) is especially protected and is not generally known to the public. This usually is a matter of classifying and marking information with an appropriate protective caveat such as "secret" or "high business impact." Then there has to be a value, an economic benefit. This is where you use the information concerning the amount of money that was invested and the amount of business that could be lost if the trade secret were compromised to a competitor that used it. Finally, there is a "reasonableness" test. The questions to be answered include: "Has the company taken measures to protect these trade secrets?" "Are these measures reasonable for the value of the trade secret?" Some benchmarking might be needed to answer the latter question. Finally, has the cost/benefit analysis determined?

When you have determined the criticality/business impact and the value of the sensitive information you can then work to determine if existing security practices provide the protection it warrants. If enhanced security measures are needed, you have some of the key information needed to do a cost/benefit analysis. Now you are truly ready to design appropriate countermeasures and determine a cost/benefit analysis for those countermeasures.

While it is difficult to determine the adverse impact of business espionage, some rather astounding numbers have emerged from a number of studies. A great deal of the current estimated economic losses attributed to business espionage are based on surveys and estimates by various government agencies, quasi-government agencies, academia, and security experts. This is due in part to the fact that business espionage is not necessarily a crime in some countries. But even more importantly it is because even where it is a crime (such as in the United States), many businesses do not want to report losses to business espionage because it could undermine the value of the company, its

[2]World Trade Organization Trade-Related Aspects of Intellectual Property Rights (TRIPS), http://www.wto.org/english/tratop_e/trips_e/t_agm3_e.htm

stock prices, brand, and reputation. As a result, the numbers vary considerably. But regardless of whether you take the lowest estimates or the highest estimates—and the best practice is probably to take an average—the numbers are astoundingly large and appear to be growing.

For example, the U.S. Commerce Department estimates that the annual intellectual property theft loss topped $250 billion a year for businesses in the United States during 2010. This means, for example, that intellectual property losses cost the United States at least 750,000 jobs in the same period, according to the U.S. Commerce Department.[3]

Furthermore, the International Chamber of Commerce puts the global fiscal loss attributed to intellectual property theft at more than US$600 billion a year.[4] The National (U.S.) Intellectual Property Law Enforcement Council did an extensive survey and put losses in one month at more than US$250 billion globally. At that rate, the business losses would be US$3 trillion a year, although the council estimates it is more likely half that, or realistically about US$1.5 trillion a year.[5]

Other countries and organizations have different estimates. The British Broadcasting Company said a study they did indicated global business losses to industrial espionage exceeded US$300 billion a year in 2012. The British MI5 security agency reported that one incident alone cost a British company more than US$1.2 billion and they say the annual business spying losses within the United Kingdom, by itself, were estimated at more than US$16 billion in 2012.[6] The Canadian Security and Intelligence Services (CSIS) put the losses to business spying for Canadian businesses at between US$50-150 billion a year in 2011.[7] The CSIS opined that the lack of a law to make business espionage illegal contributed to Canada becoming an easy place to target a company's Trade Secrets. According to Peter Schweizer, in *Foreign Affairs* magazine, the Australian Security and Intelligence Organization has estimated that Australian companies lose close to US$3 billion a year to intellectual property theft. Germany counterintelligence

[3] Cheryl D. Smith, "How Pervasive Is it?" U.S. Chamber of Commerce Global Intellectual Property Center, November, 2011, http://www.theglobalipcenter.com.
[4] Christopher Burgess and Richard Power, CIO, July 10, 2006; http://www.cio.com/article.2445646/security
[5] The Report of the Commission on the Theft of American Intellectual Property, February 2013; http://www.ipcommission.org/report/IP _Commission_Report_052213. House
[6] Hearings before U.S. House of Representatives SubComitee on Counterterrorism and Intelligence, June 28, 2012 in Washington, D.C.
[7] 6-NBC News, November 30, 2011, http://www.cbc.ca/news/canada

officials have said the country's intellectual property losses are estimated to be in excess of US$80 billion, which they note, translates to at least 30,000 German jobs.

Recently the Center for Strategic and International Studies completed a study with help from McAfee, the computer security company. The director of technology and public policy, Andrew Lewis, challenged a US$1 trillion figure McAfee had cited based on the results of its surveys. Lewis criticized the survey methodology and instead recommended using actual economic modeling. As a result, the center found the losses to be between US$20 billion and US$140 billion, and pegged the job losses at 508,000 globally.[8] This modeling was based on models used to estimate the economic effects of threats such as car crashes and ocean piracy. They then tailored their study to business espionage The problem with that approach is that intellectual property losses are not the same as a car crash—where the vehicle has a known value and is reported to law enforcement—and even piracy where hijacked products on a ship have a known quantity and value based on a manifest. Because of this, many experts argue these figures are low for the U.S. when it comes to intellectual property, with all its economic nuances and reporting issues. In many ways it is like comparing apples and oranges, especially when you consider that this study was focused on the cyber-losses, which are only a fraction of the total losses resulting from business espionage. Even though this is the lowest figure that has surfaced, the losses are still extremely high.

Regardless of the exact amount, it is important to understand the significance of annual global business losses to business spying that are potentially close to, or in excess of, a trillion US dollars a year worldwide. Add to that job losses that may exceed a million jobs worldwide, these losses are significant. And as most everyone realizes, the threat of business espionage is continuing to grow.

A 2008 survey of more than 7000 CEOs, CFOs, CIO, CSOs, and vice president/directors in some 119 countries conducted by PriceWaterhouseCoopers entitled "Safeguarding the New Currency of Business" focused on cyber-security. According to the survey, "When data breaches occur, they hurt." A significant percentage of respondents cited negative business impacts from the loss of their intellectual property, including financial losses (nearly 40%), and nearly a third reported damage to their brand and reputation. As the title indicates the study also reported that,

---

[8] "Study: Cybercrime Tally Way Off," *Tampa Tribune*, July 29, 2013.

"Information has become the new currency of business—and its portability, accessibility and mobility back and forth across international, corporate and organizational boundaries are crucial components of a collaborative globally connected business world."[9]

In spite of these numbers, as was noted earlier, employee theft is ranked way above business espionage as a concern of business, yet the American Management Association puts losses due to theft at less than US$200 billion a year.[10] While this number is significant, it is nowhere near the global losses experienced due to business espionage. As for business continuity, the most expensive hurricane in U.S. history, Hurricane Katrina, centered in New Orleans, is estimated to have cost between US$108 billion.[11] All of these threats ended up more significant than business spying in the Securitas survey of Fortune 1000 companies but losses attributed to business espionage are at least that much and are probably several times greater than threats attributed to natural disasters and internal theft combined.

The obvious question is, "How can the losses due to business spying be so severe business yet leaders are apparently so unaware of the impact?" Obviously, businesses need to look closely at the business espionage threat, the business impact of espionage losses, and then make decisions that include reducing the overall risk business spying poses.

Another way to help decide on what needs to be protected is to determine what types of information have been stolen by business spies in the past. Historical data can help to determine what information your business has that could be of interest to business spies. This book has discussed a number of case studies and examples that will help. A survey of Fortune 1000 companies disclosed that the following types of information had been targeted:

- Sales forecast and strategic plans
- Client information and customer lists
- Financial information
- Organizational plans
- Research data
- Design library information

---

[9] "Safeguarding the New Currency of Business," PricewaterhouseCoopers study, October, 2008.

[10] Karen Ott Mayer, "How to Guard Against Employee Theft," *Houston Business Journal*, March 9, 2012.

[11] Eric S. Blake, Christopher W. Landsea, Ethan J. Gibney, "The Deadliest, Costliest and Most Intense United States Tropical Cyclones" National Hurricane Center, August 2011.

- Product information
- Manufacturing processes and recipes
- Personnel information[12]

Of that information, companies were asked to estimate the value of information lost to business espionage. The participating companies reported that the loss of strategic plans costs the most at about US$1.4 billion; the loss of research and development related data was valued at US$1.35 billion; the loss of manufacturing process related information was valued at US$566 million; the loss marketing plans was valued at US$460 million; the loss intellectual property was valued at US$440 million; the loss of financial information was valued at US$360 million; the loss of information about upcoming mergers and acquisitions was valued at US$179 million; the loss of customer lists were valued at US$167 million; and the loss of personnel information was valued at US$114 million.[13]

---

[12] Kathleen Ohlson, "Survey: Fortune 1000 Companies Losing Billions in Stolen Information," CNN, September 28, 1999. http://www.cnn.com/tech/computing/9909/28/fortune.1K.idg

[13] Ibid.

9

PHYSICAL AND PERSONNEL SECURITY COUNTERMEASURES

Business Espionage
© 2015 Elsevier Inc. All rights reserved.

Abstract

This chapter focuses on all the physical and security counter-measures that can and should be used by companies to protect their sensitive business information from spying. It is a comprehensive look at physical and security countermeasures employed by governments and companies. It also explains how implementing these countermeasures lowers the vulnerabilities and the business espionage risk.

Introduction

While everyone is always looking for an all-encompassing solution that will end all worries about business espionage, so far, no one has found one. And, after more than 40 years of looking for it myself, I am convinced there is no one "magic solution." The answer to countering business-spying threats is the same as countering other security threats: develop strong risk-based overlapping and comprehensive countermeasures to threats. This will lower your vulnerabilities and ensure your business is prepared to deal with the inevitable and diverse business threats of today.

In some ways I think countermeasures (Chapters 9, 10, and 11) are the most important part of this book because, as noted in the discussion on the risk assessment process, strengthening security and lowering vulnerabilities is the best way to lower your security risk. And, if we do not lower our risk to business espionage threat, this whole process has very little value. But it is also important to know the major threats, their likelihood of occurrence, and the *modus operandi* most often used, which means making protective measure decisions based on the holistic threats.

Clearly one thing everyone needs to do is look at the best practices and physical/personnel security standards for effectively countering business espionage. There are security standards for supply chains, banks, water systems, chemical plants, and food industries, and associations such as the ASIS International have general physical security standards, while other associations such as the Transported Asset Protection Association (TAPA) have physical security standards for various sectors, including transportation. But there are not a lot of specified standards for protection from business espionage. The closest standards that have specific objectives related to information protection are set out in ISO 17799, but these are also oriented more toward the IT world, basically ignoring non-IT related threats and vulnerabilities. However, there are a number of accepted standards for physical security, and even though they are based on other threats, they can be invaluable in protecting against business spying. Many physical security standards apply to a number of security threats, including business-spying threats.

In this chapter, we will also look back at the case studies discussed in earlier chapters during this analysis and use them to identify the threats and *modus operandi*. We will then we can examine the vulnerabilities that allowed the threats to be successful. The key, then, is to develop countermeasures that will reduce those typical vulnerabilities and protect the business enterprise from the identified threats. I believe that the espionage committed in all my case studies and examples could have been prevented. Therefore, we will strive to set out principles that can help to prevent spies from successfully targeting businesses. In the rare case where it would have been exceptionally difficult to prevent an attack, countermeasures could still have been implemented to reduce the adverse business impact (consequences) of the spying attack.

As noted, there is no "magic solution," and no single security strategy can prevent every business spying attack. There is also no perfect set of countermeasures, and any truly effective counterespionage program cannot be fixed and static as threats are constantly evolving and new vulnerabilities emerging. What protected you last year might not work as well this year. The threat vectors will be probing and trying to find new techniques so the countermeasures employed must be dynamic and constantly adjusting to the threat. There are also accidents and mistakes that must also be handled.

Even if you have your access control measures in place so it is very difficult for a human being to get into a controlled area, spies will try and use small remote-controlled devices flying through the air to bypass traditional physical security measures such as fences and gates. Now you have to adjust your security countermeasures. If you find the threat is coming from robotic cleaning services and the equipment they use, then you have to adjust countermeasures again. The process is ongoing and never truly ends.

When we talk about business espionage countermeasures, another term that can be used is risk management. The countermeasures we recommend will allow a business to manage the risk. While sometimes it may be necessary to accept a vulnerability or a consequence/business impact this should be an enterprise decision, and the business should manage the risk rather than just react to it.

One of the major factors in any risk management program or countermeasures approach is the cost. This can be calculated by looking at the amount of the security equipment that needs to be purchased and the security personnel that need to be hired or contracted. It may also involve the time taken away from operational activities by your employees for, among other things, their security-related education and awareness training. If the potential adverse consequences, based on the critical impact assets that are identified, are lower than the potential cost, that countermeasure is not cost effective. The good news is that many of the most effective countermeasures do not cost that much and many of the recommended countermeasures also provide enhanced security for other significant threats such as theft, workplace violence, and fraud.

Business Espionage Security Awareness Training

Without a doubt, one of the most effective things any company can do to protect its business secrets and sensitive information is to have a workforce that is educated and aware of business espionage threat. I have seen this attitude often, but if the leadership and workforce view business spying as one of those "James Bond" threats that only occur in the movies, there will be major vulnerabilities. I have delivered very few training sessions where I did not have someone in the company come up after the training to share a story about an incident, and how they now recognize that the incident may have involved someone using a business-spying technique.

It is important to understand that the security aspect of a company cannot protect everything by themselves. It is an established principle in security and law enforcement that law enforcement agencies need the public to report what they see and private security entities need the general employees of companies to be the reporting eyes and ears. Without that support law enforcement or security will not be nearly as effective as they could be if they were teamed up with all company employees. It must be clear that the security of a company's sensitive information is the responsibility of every employee, not just those with "security" in their job title. Therefore, you cannot give some of the security responsibility to employees without empowering them with the knowledge of what they should be alert for and how to respond if they see or experience the possible threat.

In the U.S. Air Force, while stationed in Berlin, Germany, I was credited with having the best counterespionage education and awareness program in the entire Air Force. Our objective in the Air Force was to brief 100 percent of an installation's personnel. My objective in Berlin was to brief, and otherwise educate, 400 percent of the Air Force population in Berlin (meaning I tried to ensure every employee was briefed four times a year). Many thought that was overkill even in what most acknowledged as the spy capital of the world at the time. We used bulletin boards, computer notes, wallet-sized cards, library displays, newspaper ads, and articles, and we delivered four different kinds of training each year. This included standard threat briefings, methods/techniques briefings, and what-to-do briefings. It also included bringing a former double agent in to provide a briefing on what it was like to work as a spy for the Soviet and East German intelligence services. As a result, the Air Force in Berlin had the highest number of active espionage cases ever uncovered at a single geographic location. Even special penetration tests against sensitive targets by U.S. Air Force penetration teams were detected and neutralized in record time. Was that because we were that good, or was it because we were just lucky? No! I have no doubt that our success in countering espionage in Berlin was due to the involvement of Air Force personnel throughout Berlin and their regular reports of suspected espionage or possible threats. They were involved because we worked hard to keep them educated and aware. They knew what to look for and what to do if they saw it. My experience is that the majority of employees will do this if they are properly educated and motivated.

Some of the so-called counterespionage education and awareness programs I have reviewed are no more than a review of existing security-related policies and procedures. Such an approach has little or no lasting value. Others are speeches that focus on penalties and consequences. Again, this is not effective and these programs leave employees saying the company's counterespionage program is almost worthless.

Some will maintain that threatening people with punishment is counterproductive. While it certainly should not be the main thrust of your education and awareness program, depending on how you define "threatening" it may be one of the many subjects that should be addressed. Employees need to know the company takes protection of its sensitive information and trade secrets very seriously and will take appropriate legal and/or other action against anyone who is involved in the theft or compromise of their sensitive information. As we saw from looking at the case studies on the motivation of spies, if they think a company is not really serious about protecting its secrets, they will be more likely to engage in espionage and will rationalize that the company security is weak because the company does not really care. A good education and awareness program will not come across as a threat, but it will make it clear the company is very serious about protecting itself.

Key Elements of a Good Employee Counterespionage Education and Awareness Program

I am frequently asked what would constitute a good counterespionage security and awareness program. Once again, there is no "one-size-fits-all" solution, but the following are some of the key elements of a good education and awareness program for business espionage:

- Make sure employees understand that the senior leadership of the company strongly supports this program and expects them to do the same (having a leader introduce the training in person, or on video, and/or a letter from the president/CEO can help drive this point home).
- Make sure employees understand the threat of business spying is real; use real examples (many are provided in this book).
- Explain the different kinds of threats and the variety of methods used in business spying (employees say this helped them to spot a social engineering attempt, for example).
- Explain the value of the company's sensitive information and the damage it could cause if the information is lost (make the loss personal by noting how many jobs or bonuses could be lost).
- Explain how to identify sensitive, classified, or high-impact information (whichever term you use).
- Explain what employees are supposed to be alert for, sensitive to, and why.
- Explain how employees can report spying attempts or even suspicions (stress that they do not have to have what they might consider proof before they make a report; you want them to report even suspicions). Normal channels include, as appropriate, reporting to supervisors, reporting to security, reporting via an anonymous-capable hotline or email, etc.

In addition, I recommend specialized counterespionage education and awareness programs. One of the most important is a counterespionage program that is linked to travel security and includes a focus on business-spying threats, especially in high-threat locations.

Other important and valuable specialized programs include tailored training for receptionists, administrative personnel, human resources staff, IT staff, sales and marketing staff, research and development staff, operations staff, senior leadership, and security personnel. The more training each of these functions get that is geared toward the threats faced and the methods used for their job and location, the more likely they will be able to spot, report, and defeat the threat attempts.

It is worth noting that many companies like to "cover" their security education and awareness at the new employee orientation program briefings, but then believe no additional training is needed. This is a serious mistake. While new employees should definitely get their trained on the company's counterespionage program, the training cannot stop here. For one thing, new employees have repeatedly told me they are on "information overload" at orientation and they do not have the perspective they will have after being on the job for a while. Plus, threats are evolving and changing. Therefore, it is important that training not just be for new employees.

Counterespionage training should be held for all employees on a regular basis, especially for those that have access to sensitive information. Additionally, specialized training should be given to functions that are commonly targeted during business-spying attempts. Of course, awareness training cannot stop at awareness. It must include what to do when employees suspect business espionage, which is where a comprehensive reporting program comes into play.

Business Espionage Reporting Program

As mentioned in the preceding section, awareness is important but it is of limited value if employees are not using that awareness to detect potential threats and to respond appropriately, reporting to the head of the company's counterespionage program.

With today's technology there are a number of potential ways to report concerns. Probably the most important aspect is that employees report anything with possible (not just "confirmed") business-spying ties as quickly as possible to the counter business espionage head That can be by telephone, by computer, by text, etc. It is often good to have a special "hotline" that operates 24 hours-a-day, 7 days-a-week.

Whatever reporting methods you rely on, it is important that employees in the company know the telephone number, email address, etc., that should be used. It is also important to think about the potential for reporting this anonymously if there is a fear of "getting involved" or "retaliation." It is also important to think about the potential of alerting spies so they can cover their activities and possibly avoid being caught. The first objective is to know but if you can get the reporting individual or entity to think about how to report and not alert the spies, that is best.

For example, if you are concerned about someone monitoring the telephone system, it would be good to use a cell phone or another phone outside the office to make a call to the counterespionage contact person. Sitting at your desk and saying your office could be "bugged" is probably not the best way to make that concern known. Sending an email when someone believes the IT systems may have been hacked may also not be the best way to report a penetration concern. Once again, this requires education and awareness so that employees find it easy and a priority to report but get their concern reported quickly and securely.

It is also important that the reporting methods also be easy to use, allow for confidentiality, and be as timely as possible. It is also important that these reporting methods be widely known through education and awareness programs that include things like online and bulletin board posts, newsletters, sign boards, wallet-sized cards, pay statement notes, etc. They should also be integrated into all education/awareness presentations.

Travel Security Program that Includes Business Espionage Threat

This topic was discussed in Chapter 6, but the vulnerability of employees to business espionage as they travel is so important that it warrants being addressed in detail as a countermeasure. Currently a number of companies are concerned enough about their employees safety and security that they have a travel security program put in place to educate employees about travel to areas where physical threats might be high. There are a number of companies that provide travel security information to their traveling employees, which includes daily summaries of threats around the world. These services normally address threats from terrorism, civil disturbances, crime, even weather and health, but I can say that none of the top 10 (by volume of users) security daily reports/travel security programs address business espionage adequately. Most do not ever address business spying at all and those that do, do it very infrequently and incompletely. Usually it is included in a "special report" if addressed at all. While these services would quickly report a drive-by shooting or suicide bomber and have also become good at reporting certain IT losses, travelers have no idea whether their hotel room could be bugged and searched or if their driver might be recording their internal conversations. They do not know if the company they are dealing with and the hotel they are staying in are working together with government intelligence services to steal any and all business information. The bottom line is this: If you do not have a travel security program that specifically evaluates business espionage threat and provides examples and updates, you should get another travel security program service and make it clear that information on the business-spying threat is one of your requirements. Educated customers will force these travel security information providers to do what they should have been doing all along, which is to prepare travelers for the substantial business espionage threats they will face when they travel.

Closely linked to and sometimes overlapping the travel security program is the importance of requiring all employees to get advanced clearance of any papers written/published and any presentations being made in any forums around the world. If travel to an international forum is approved and the information to be presented is cleared, it is still wise to put the conference or program into a business-spying context and make certain the employee knows that this is a forum where someone could attempt to elicit further information from him/her. This kind of preparation is important to help deter and prevent effective business-spying targeting.

Executive Protection

Also closely linked to the counterespionage travel security program is any executive protection program the company might have. Executive protection programs also tend to focus on physical security and protecting executives from physical threats, but it is also important to understand that senior executives will be attractive targets for business espionage, including their executive offices, their homes, and their aircraft, vehicles, or hotel rooms when traveling or in transit. Since all of these provide an opportunity to spy on a company executive and gain knowledge of sensitive information it is important that counterespionage be incorporated into executive protection programs.

A TSCM sweep could be as important as a bomb-detection sweep. All the concerns about working from home, IT security, and trash covers apply to the executive's home and especially to his/her vehicles, aircraft, and hotel rooms. Incorporating counterespionage measures and education/awareness training is an important part of executive protection. Executive protection is not just protection from physical harm, but protection from any potentially adverse acts or results that involve the executive.

All too often, security is afraid to approach senior executives with this kind of threat-awareness information. Yet senior executives may be some of the most significant sources of extremely sensitive information. Therefore, if your executive protection program is all about "body guards" you might not be that skilled in protecting sensitive information from compromise, a major vulnerability in an executive protection approach.

Clear, Demonstrated Senior Leadership Support

One of the most important things that can make a counterespionage program more effective is to make it clear that the most senior leadership of the company supports the program and agrees it is vitally important. Letters, emails, and videos or opening remarks by the CEO and/or president or similar level/titled senior leader are very important because it conveys a message to the entire company about the importance of protecting the company's business secrets.

If the senior leaders (CEO, president, etc.) refer to some of the specific counterespionage security measures that are important, employees will take notice. For example, when company security procedures dictate wearing the company identification badge and challenging those without one, a CEO who prominently and always displays his/her ID badge and challenges people not displaying their badge will strengthen the security of the company by doing so. If, on the other hand, the CEO or president says "everyone should know me" and refuses to wear his/her company photo ID, most of the staff will decide they do not need to wear their IDs either. In no time the policy/procedure will be worthless. While most senior leaders will provide some level of verbal support, this is not a true investment of time and effort, and it also communicates loudly and clearly to staff that the counterespionage program is not that important.

While this is not a terribly expensive part of an effective program, it is a symbolically important and essential step. I call it the blessing or mandate "from on high." It is important for an effective program, let alone for protecting the sensitive information executives routinely deal with.

Identifying and Properly Classifying Sensitive Information

It is important for those of us in security to understand that in order to run an effective and efficient business, information must be exchanged within the organization and with partners, clients, and suppliers. However, this does not mean that every bit of information in an enterprise should be equally shared with all other entities within or outside of the company. Remember the security principle discussed previously: You cannot protect everything, so it is important to determine what is important and warrants protection, which is closely linked to the potential adverse consequence if the information were compromised (there probably should be several levels of classification of information and data).

In the U.S. government/military there are four major classification categories:

1. For Official Use Only—for internal use but with limited damage if compromised; minimal controls.
2. Confidential—information whose unauthorized disclosure could cause damage to national security and must be protected.
3. Secret—information whose unauthorized disclosure could result in serious damage to national security and requires a higher level of protection.
4. Top Secret—information whose unauthorized disclosure could result in exceptionally grave danger to the nation and requires the highest levels of protection.

While there were once special categories of top secret information and caveats such as "no foreign release" or special code words attached to some information, the gist of these major categories relates to potential damage to national security. Classifications used in business should be similarly based on the potential damage to a business.

Several companies I have dealt with have used the same three categories—confidential, secret, and top secret—with an emphasis on the degree of danger to the enterprise's business. Another company I have worked with uses three categories that are linked to the potential adverse impact on the enterprise if the information were compromised; they use "high business impact," "medium business impact," and "low business impact," which are self-explanatory. Yet another company uses: Routine (meaning it is already known and is open-source data), vital (meaning it is important and the loss would hurt but the business could survive), and critical (meaning that the success and future of the company is directly linked to this information). This has allowed this particular company to focus on protecting its most critical sensitive information in terms of the adverse business impact.

In all of these examples, the focus is on the potential adverse impact if this information were compromised/lost. Would there be some damage, serious damage, or exceptionally grave damage? Answering that question is the key to determining the classification level. Then, of course, any documents or materials should be marked accordingly and the protection afforded should increase as the criticality goes up.

Some companies have come up with other terms that are linked to legal terminology such as "trade secret" or "proprietary information." It is not important what label you put on the information as long as it reflects the value and sensitivity of the information and its potential adverse business impact if compromised. However, it is important that the meaning of each label is known throughout the enterprise. It might be helpful to work with a law firm that has both the personnel and intellectual property expertise to come up with the best terms and caveats for your particular business enterprise and country of origin.

The objective is to be able to determine what information you must protect from competition and then to focus on the highest level of protection to help prevent the most potential adverse business impact. Protection must include limiting the number of individuals who have access to highest business impact information and what protection must be given to those handling and using that information. Obviously this also means including the classification and protective measures in your counterespionage education and awareness program.

When you go through the important process of determining which of your assets have the biggest potential adverse business impact if lost, this is also an ideal time (and this should logically be a part of the determination process) to determine and assign a value to those assets. How much is the information or asset worth? How much research and development time and cost was invested? How much marketing will be/has been invested? How much have you spent to protect this information/asset? What would be the amount of money you could lose in business if a competitor had this hard-earned information and used it to compete with you? Knowing the value and having a process to determine that value is important because it is required by some state and federal laws (i.e., for trade secrets to be valued). It also can help you decide about the cost/benefit for protective measures.

As we have said before, you do not want to spend more for protective measures than the information/asset is worth, but if, for example, protecting an asset costs US$50,000, but it is valued at more than US$50 million, there is a pretty clear cost/benefit rationale for investing in the protective measures needed to do so.

Another important aspect of this process is that many of the criminal and civil protections provided in jurisdictions that have such protection require that information/resources compromised be properly marked/identified legally to qualify for this protection.

The key is to have a process to identify, and the regularly review and update, the sensitivity and value of business information. As business decisions are made to invest in research and development, new products/services, new locations, new manufacturing sites, mergers and acquisitions, etc., it is important that these business decisions are properly evaluated in terms of the value and sensitivity. All resources, and associated information, should be protected according to their potential adverse impact and cost to the company. This includes government and regulatory requirements. All of this should be done upfront and not after the resource has been compromised or valuable information lost.

Include in Business Continuity/Disaster Recovery Plans

Just like business travelers who are prepared for traditional physical security threats such as terrorism, theft, workplace violence, severe weather, or natural disasters, many companies have some kind of business continuity and disaster recovery plans in place. However, most of the plans I have reviewed do not address the potentially catastrophic losses that can occur if business espionage succeeds and the company's most sensitive information and trade secrets are lost.

It is important that business continuity and disaster recovery plans incorporate business espionage threat and make disaster recovery and business continuity plans to address it should it occur. This kind of planning will also help to drive home the importance of making every effort to prevent a successful business-spying attack because the consequences and adverse business impact will be addressed beforehand. This is where decisions can be considered regarding legal recourse or working with authorities for possible criminal prosecutions, if that option is available.

Conduct a Holistic Risk Assessment

One of the best ways to start building a good counterespionage program is to avoid the temptation to just start "throwing" security measures out and implementing them because "that's what security does." The typical security response is to get a few guards, put up a fence, install CCTV cameras, and institute some type of access control. Another common tactic is to use security measures that other companies have implemented. Instead of those approaches, when determining the countermeasures needed, start with a good, solid, holistic risk assessment that addresses all threats, including business espionage and the likelihood of its occurrence. Then look at established company standards and do a vulnerability assessment that addresses physical, personnel, and IT security in a synergistic manner. Finally, do a consequence/business impact assessment and know what and where the most sensitive information is located. Protect that first and foremost. When you put all of these components together into a risk assessment, you can design a countermeasures program that will be effective for your particular business. While your security program should be tailored to your particular circumstances, remember that it will only be a "snapshot" of time it was done. Threats, vulnerabilities, and consequences are always changing so you will want to do risk assessments on a regular basis. Do not accept anything less than a complete risk assessment that addresses all threats and their likelihood of occurrence, any gaps and vulnerabilities present within the company, as well as the possible consequences.

Well-Constructed, Comprehensive Security Policies and Procedures

It is important to have good, sound security policies and procedures as one of those fundamental building blocks to a good counterespionage program. In this context security policies will be formal, high-level statements or plans that embrace the goals and objectives of the enterprise. These include concepts we have addressed such as the principle that every employee is responsible for organizational security, as well as the idea that the least access necessary to conduct business is the best. To establish and promote these goals and objectives, you need policies, standards, and procedures in place.

Policies are mandatory and are defined by standards. Standards, in turn, are mandatory actions or rules. Finally, procedures are the steps taken to accomplish a policy goal. Procedures are the "how to" for protecting information and assets. They should All of the categories of security should be specifically addressed and include at least: access controls, registration of visitors, escort requirements, issuance, revocation and wear of identification, key control, property and removal controls, trash removal, information destruction, IT controls, information marking, classification, lock-up requirements, clean desk requirements, due diligence of business partners, hiring and termination procedures, background investigations, security education, and awareness training (new employees and recurring, specialized). These are some of the basic categories that should be addressed in an enterprise's security policies and procedures.

Additionally, policies/procedures should address a travel security program and include a process for identifying and constantly reviewing/revising high-threat locations. Travel to any high-threat environment should be carefully considered; there should be a review and approval process and mandatory training to deal with the environment being visited. This might include advanced briefings/training for travelers to high-threat environments and a debriefing of travelers returning from high-threat environments. The U.S. military and government has implemented these procedures since the Cold War days for any travel to a high threat (in those days "Communist controlled") country.

All of these policies and procedures should be reviewed and approved by legal counsel, and they should be regularly reviewed and revised as appropriate.

Create a Specific and Focused Information Protection Team

The company should also establish an entity, a kind of information protection team, responsible for the company's information protection/counterespionage program. This team should be multi-dimensional and multi-functional. Some of the roles typically held on such a team include:

- Senior leadership representation
- Operations
- Legal
- Human resources
- IT (covering computer use, server rooms, telephone lines, mobile devices, etc.)
- Security
- Facilities
- Finance

- Procurement/Contracting
- Research and development (if appropriate)
- Event planners (if appropriate)
- Marketing (an opportunity to review all marketing materials, approaches)
- Sales
- Whoever is responsible for coordinating travel

Do Comprehensive Due Diligence of Partners, Suppliers, Vendors, and Clients

Due diligence is a concept that focuses on legal concepts to shield claims of negligence. When it comes to information protection it is a different concept. Too many companies consider due diligence only when it comes to business partners, suppliers, and vendors as it relates to legal registration and finances. While these are important, they are not necessarily the only or even the most important aspects of due diligence in the protection of sensitive information. In this context, due diligence is the process under which prospective relationships can be evaluated with respect to the potential for adverse consequences. Before entering into a business relationship with another organization, proper inquiries should be made to determine the suitability of the partnering organization and its elements or associates. This is especially important because it generally involves some sharing of proprietary information. In fact, in my experience, a large number of losses occurred when joint ventures, outsourcing, or subcontracting were involved. All too often we only did the level of due diligence that should have been undertaken before—after problems surfaced. In one case, when it was apparent there were some major intellectual property losses occurring, a client asked for due diligence on all their suppliers. We found that 75 percent of the suppliers were either owned by, or were affiliated with, their principal competitor. It is no wonder that company is not among the top in their industry and nearly went bankrupt in 2014.

At least seven types of information are warranted in due diligence as it relates to information protection:

1. Financial and performance metrics
2. Legal standing
3. Reputation including IPR violations, trade complaints, and expert-control issues
4. Potential links or ties with firms that are competitors, have IPR violations, trade complaints, or export-control issues
5. Ties to foreign-owned enterprises

6. Information security experience and expertise
7. Willingness to commit to and allow unannounced audits for compliance to security standards

At least all of these categories should be pursued in detail. This is more than the traditional due diligence done by most companies, but it will pay major dividends in preventing problems in the future.

Be Involved in Office/Site Location Selection

Closely linked with the due diligence concept for partners, suppliers, and contractors is doing a security risk assessment/due diligence on any office, production, or logistics related sites. While things like size, location, and price are obviously important selection criteria, it is also important to have information security and counterespionage elements involved in the selection process to ensure the company has considered all aspects and the total risk before making the ultimate decision on where they will locate. Additionally, it is important to have this aspect addressed in any contracts, requiring immediate notification if any listed competitor is expected to be in a building or on a site, at which point the contract would become null and void.

This is also true of selecting senior executive housing, expatriate housing abroad, meeting sites for important board, management, or sales gatherings and selecting law firms, accounting firms, and security or other service providers.

Since this is a dynamic aspect of business, it is important that this kind of counterespionage due diligence be ongoing and regularly reviewed to ensure there have not been changes, mergers, acquisitions, etc., that could impact information-related security.

Conduct Background Investigations/Personnel Security

It is also important to have a good process in place for conducting background investigations and other screenings for employees because my experience has shown that roughly 70 percent of problems encountered in business espionage involve or are somehow connected to employees and contractors. This process should include good background investigations and screening of employees that addresses issues potentially related to business spying.

Each location/jurisdiction might have slightly different laws and rules governing pre-employment and post-employment background investigations and screening, but ideally you should have an ongoing background investigation process in place. There should be regular background investigations of personnel with access to sensitive business information, because people's situations and backgrounds change. Most places have security background investigation services that together with other security measures can be used to enhance security for all types of sensitive information.

Some of the minimum information that should be included in screening or background investigations includes:

- Criminal history checks
- Driving records and history
- Drug tests
- Credit history
- Employment history and education verifications
- "Developed" references, which generally have more credence than one an individual provides on this own

Have the provided source provide the names and contact information for five more people that know your background investigation subject. Consider asking for another three to five names from this second layer. By the time you get three layers out from the self-provided references, you probably have a good idea if there are any problems. Hopefully, human resources, hopefully working together with security and legal personnel and those responsible for information security, have processes in place so the company does not easily hire someone who is being "planted" in the company by competitors. Likewise, the company should not hire someone who based on his/her background poses a major potential threat for compromise. Screening programs have to take protection of sensitive information into consideration as a part of the hiring process, and those doing the screening must have training and expertise on how to evaluate background and testing results.

For example, it is important to include credit checks/investigation, whenever possible, in screening individuals who will have access to sensitive information. Credit checks and investigations can also uncover important clues as to whether job applicants/employees may be susceptible to recruitment through the MICE or CRIME principles (discussed in earlier chapters). Evidence of large credit card balances and late payments is frequently indicative of a lifestyle that exceeds means, something that often makes applicants/employees desperate enough to commit acts of economic espionage or other trade secret piracy in exchange for the monetary rewards offered to them by competitors and foreign governments. An analysis of credit card receipts/spending can sometimes reveal (a) behavioral proclivities of applicants/employees that may be exploitable through sexual entrapment and compromise, and (b) evidence of extensive travel that provides opportunity for agent recruitment activities (money, ego, or ideology) by government spy agencies, competitors, or professional investigators. It is worth noting that prior to allegedly disclosing the trade secrets of his employer (Avery Dennison) to Four Pillars, Victor Lee made a large number of trips to Taiwan under the guise of family business, academic speaking engagements, and consulting activities.[1] Proactive monitoring of his credit card activities by security and/or finance personnel might have revealed the extensiveness of these travel activities and triggered a subsequent security evaluation. This might have permitted Avery Dennison to remind Mr. Lee of the legal responsibilities and potential penalties associated with failure to comply with his nondisclosure agreement. This could, potentially, have deterred his business-spying activities prior to the loss of sensitive information and trade secrets.

For those employees who will have access to the most sensitive information it is also worthwhile to consider "enhanced" background investigations on immediate family members as well. Especially in Latin America and Asia, family ties are among the most important relationships one can have. It is good to know if a father, spouse, son/daughter, etc., works for a government agency, competitor, or a company that supplies or contracts with a competitor. This can mean a potential conflict of interest and should be known and considered as a part of the hiring process, or can be discovered during the regular background checks of existing key employees.

Remember to also look at where individuals have lived and where they were educated. This can be one area to address in pre-employment interviews and investigations. Additionally, knowing that money is a motivator, also look for any signs of undue affluence.

There are also other screening tools that can be of value when personnel have access to critically important information. Integrity and other testing programs can be of value to lower the likelihood of hiring someone who should never have been given access to critically important and sensitive business secrets.

When screening is discussed, the use of a polygraph examination often comes up. Depending on where the employee resides and the citizenship of employees, a polygraph may or may not be a viable screening tool. While I believe it has limited value as

---

[1] Ira Winkler, *Corporate Espionage*, Prima Publishing, 1997.

a screening mechanism, I believe that with a good examiner, the polygraph can be a valuable tool in interviewing individuals about a specific matter.

In my experience a polygraphs is only as good as the polygrapher administering the examination and interpreting the data. In reality, the polygraph is not invincible. Some experts will argue that you cannot "beat" a polygraph but you can "beat" an examiner. The bottom line to me, as a user of this tool, is that it should not be used as a major screening device, but it can be a valuable tool, where legal, in after-the-fact investigations and as a "deterrent." It is always good to remember the famous comment that Richard Nixon, then President of the United States made when he said, "Polygraph them all. I don't know anything about polygraphs and I don't know how accurate they are but I know they'll scare the hell out of people."[2]

The overall utility of polygraphs in counterespionage programs is limited by the (a) validity of the technology, (b) legal restrictions governing their use, and (c) reactive manner in which they are frequently used by security personnel. In this latter instance, security personnel use polygraphs to identify people responsible for compromising trade secrets or sensitive information after the fact. When used in this manner, polygraphs cannot be viewed as an adequate substitute for comprehensive security approaches that actively detect business spying, but they can provide a potential deterrent and demonstrate that a company takes protection of their sensitive information very seriously.

Use of polygraphs in personnel actions has significantly declined due to the passage of restrictive government laws and regulations. In place of the polygraph, many companies have substituted the use of integrity testing. "Integrity tests are designed to help identify job applicants who are likely to engage in employee theft and other undesirable behavior, such as on-the-job violence, illicit drug abuse, and disciplinary problems."[3] These tests are designed to reduce the threats of business spying through the use of an honesty hurdle during the selection process. Integrity testing methodologies generally consist of two types of assessment tools: (1) An overt integrity test and (2) personality-based tests. Overt measures of integrity function by focusing on an individual's proclivity toward dishonesty by determining, for example, their attitudes toward theft and the way they deal with

---

[2] Betsy Brantner Smith, "Taking the Mystery Out of the Polygraph," *Police Link*, February 4, 2010, http://policelink.monster/com/benefits/articles/10465.

[3] D.W. Arnold and J.W. Jones, "Who the Devil's Applying Now," *Security Management Magazine*, 2002.

evidence of prior theft. The Personnel Selection Inventory and The Reid Report are examples of this type of testing. Conversely, personality-based measures assess the degree to which an individual possesses various traits that are correlated with dishonesty, theft, or other undesirable behaviors. An example of this type of test is the Hogan Reliability Scale.

There are certainly some indications to support the validity of integrity tests for assessing an employee's behavioral potential for theft, dishonesty, and other undesirable behaviors. A report by Sackett and Wanek in *Personnel Psychology* notes that respondent scores on integrity tests correlated significantly with an individual's tendency to steal or be dishonest.[4]

Few jurisdictions have placed many restrictions on the use of integrity tests, provided that these tests meet requirements for validity and do not adversely impact protected groups. There is some limited evidence to indicate that there exist no significant differences in the response patterns of job applicants on these tests when compared across demographic groups.[5] However, evidence does tend to suggest that integrity testing can provide organizations with a mechanism to proactively "screen-out" job applicants who may become a potential or subsequent problem when it comes to protecting sensitive information.

Address Resignations and Terminations

Resignations and terminations can be very sensitive situations but from a counterespionage standpoint these are especially important milestones. As we have seen from our case studies, on many occasions individuals take information with them as they leave, especially if going to work for the competition. It is therefore important to recognize this threat and take as many precaution steps as possible to limit the loss of information by those leaving the company.

There are several steps that must be taken for all termination/resignation situations:
- First, everyone that is leaving should be interviewed and "debriefed" to determine why they are leaving and they should be asked if they are going to work for a company that is identified as a competitor.

---

[4] P.R. Sackett and J.E. Wanek, "New Developments in the Use of Measures of Honesty," *Personnel Psychology*, 1966.
[5] R.D. Gatewood and H.S. Field, *Human Resource Selection*, Harcourt Brace College Publishers, 1998.

- If an individual is knowingly leaving to work for a competitor or suspected competitor, it is important for HR and security to work with legal to make certain an appropriate cautionary legal document is sent to the competitor warning them about the consequences of using proprietary and classified information and trade secrets. Likewise, this should be communicated to the employee so they are thoroughly knowledgeable of what cannot be removed and/or shared with the competition. It would also include a review of what the consequences are if the employee violates this legal agreement.
- Then it is important to go back and look at what documents have been recently requested, what information has been downloaded, etc. A document inventory should be conducted and matched against sensitive documents the individual had access to or control of. It is recommended that interviews be conducted of colleagues to determine if the individual departing did anything unusual or suspicious.
- Finally, it is also important to block the access individuals have to company proprietary information in all forms. This might include physical removal of documents, an immediate stop to uncontrolled access (e.g., access ID card is removed from the system), and an end to IT and email access, including the individual's PC or laptop. It is also highly recommended that the company consider reimaging the departing individual's computer and other assigned mobile devices to see if there was any suspicious or unwarranted downloading or communication with the competition, which is best done by a business espionage expert.

Access controls

One of the more important physical security functions with direct applicability to protecting sensitive information and assets is the concept of access control. It is important to have good access controls, especially in areas where sensitive information is stored, worked on, and discussed. You want to do everything in your power to keep barriers between sensitive information and those who are not authorized access to that sensitive information.

While many companies "talk" about access control, not many have good access control systems in place. If you have unmanned, unmonitored doors there is a good chance they will occasionally be unlocked or propped open, and this compromises access control.

This is where the concept of "layered" security has special applicability. Access control is not just need at the main entrance; access controls are needed at *all* entrances/exits. At the main entrance(s) there should be a secondary barrier to prevent some-one from circumventing the initial controls. A minimum of two access control points should occur at each entrance. Likewise, there should be secondary and even tertiary barriers that further restrict unauthorized movement within a facility or complex. Those areas that have sensitive information in development, use, or storage should have further restrictions, and not all employees should have access to these areas. This is where the idea of need-to-know should be considered.

Depending on the sensitivity of information/assets, a company might consider special access areas, where there is strict control of anyone entering. No visitors would be authorized without special permission and special precautions being taken. Cleaning people, maintenance staff, even contract security might not be allowed in some of these areas…at least without a controlled escort. Some of these areas might warrant not allowing anyone in the area alone—a so-called "No Lone Zone"—which would mean a minimum of at least two cleared employees would be required within the area, especially if it is contains especially sensitive information. It could also include mandatory intrusion detection system coverage/controls and some live, monitored CCTV coverage of entrances, walkways, etc., as appropriate.

Anyone given access to these special access locations should have specific prior approval. Historically it has been proven that if access is generally granted only by management, there will be those who take their role very seriously and some who will grant access to almost anyone for any purpose. By have an information protection team in place to review each access request, you are more likely to eliminate frivolous and high-threat access. This fulfills the "limit access" requirement and is obviously, by definition, linked to access control measures.

It is also especially important that the company have a strict "no tail-gating" policy and enforce it. I have seen a lot of very poor access controls and have exploited people "being nice" by not slamming a door in my face. Unfortunately, I should not have been allowed into the building/area. It is important to establish a culture that knows that no one is allowed to follow anyone in and each employee must use the card access reader and open/close the door. If this does not seem to be working, in spite of consequences for not following these rules, the company may have to use a turnstile to force employees to enter/exit one at a time, except during a fire/emergency. One way or another, access control must be established and maintained.

Then we have already mentioned the importance of restricting access for contractors and guests/visitors, as well as those employees who are terminated or who resign.

Secure Storage and Locks

In addition to access control issues, there are other physical security measures that can be used to protect sensitive information from potential compromise, including secure storage of sensitive information/assets, locked doors and solid walls, and locked storage containers or internal barriers that can delay or slow down an intruder or spy. Procedures for using secure storage and locks might include a security checklist that must be completed at least daily, or a container list that records each and every opening and closing/locking of each container. Some containers have "red" and "green" magnets or cardboard "flags" that highlight when a container is locked (green) and when a container is unlocked (red). This allows an inspection team to quickly spot if something has been left unsecured and highlights the importance of intervening to secure an unlocked drawer or container. Another requirement might be that any documents that are classified (e.g., "high business impact" or "secret" information) must have a colored cover sheet so anyone with temporary access cannot look at or read information that is printed or is on a computer screen. Again, it also highlights this information as sensitive and needing protection.

Importance of Information Security Manager(s) as Program Contacts

It is important to consider appointing "information security managers" in the various business units that handle and control sensitive information. These individuals, and their alternates, can be responsible for regular checks to ensure that all personnel are properly marking, handling, and protecting sensitive business information. This is very different from an IT information security manager. This general information security manager is the interface between the business functions and the requirements to protect information, whether those requirements come from corporate security or IT security.

These individuals can also assist in checking and ensuring that when individuals leave their desks or work areas, they have properly secured/protected sensitive information. This is the impetus of "clean desk" policy/procedures and is closely linked to IT policies/procedures that have automatic screen savers, time logouts, and screen covers/filters. Information security managers can be an invaluable set of eyes and ears and an invaluable source of information on best and required security practices. With specialized education and awareness training they can become the "eyes and ears" of the counterespionage program and an important resource for counterespionage expertise and questions.

Document and Material Destruction/Trash Controls

Some of the most significant losses occur in the most mundane manner—accidental compromise by individuals who are uninformed about protection procedures for classified information and/or are lazy. I have found extremely sensitive information in the regular trash thousands of times around the world. Unfortunately, this includes examples of the U.S. military where I found, to my amazement, "top secret" material from every single division in the regular trash. In the corporate world the numbers are off the charts.

I have found at least a hundred electronic shredders either unplugged or being used as a storage table with all kind of things stacked on top and blocking the shredding slot. In all of these cases the message was clear—people were not using them.

In China I actually met individuals who had, in the past, specialized in assembling and gluing together strips of paper from strip shredders to try and recreate documents. I saw the results of Iranian students doing this with documents from the U.S. Embassy in Iran when "students" over ran the Embassy when the Shah was overthrown. There is even a current humorous television advertisement being used in the United States that shows a group of people urgently going through strips of shredded paper and finally assembling a child's colored picture just as the manager's daughter arrives and proudly notes her colored picture is on her father's office wall. The truth is that if you can reassemble a colored picture, you can reconstruct any sensitive information that has been strip shredded. Treating all trash as potentially sensitive and having locked containers for all waste, readily available shredder/pulverizers, and locked dumpsters can help lower the threat to waste materials that have not yet been rendered unusable.

The bottom line here is that you must have a multifaceted program to protect sensitive information from being the target of a trash cover or dumpster dive. Rather than a strip shredder, you should always employ a cross-cut shredder or pulverizer that turns paper and electronic product into small pieces that are so mixed they are much more difficult to reassemble. It is important that these shredders be available in large numbers so they are convenient. Anything that is not convenient will not be used. If you have a so-called "centralized" shredder, it will not be widely used. Instead of having a centralized box for holding classified documents, do away with regular trash containers and put locked document holders at every desk and at every printer center. People are more likely to take their personal trash (cola cans, lunch boxes, used tissues, candy wrappers, etc.) to a couple of central regular trash containers than they are to use centralized classified document bins. Understand human nature and plan to protect information in spite of our natural character flaws. I recommend a cross-cut shredder at every desk where sensitive information is in document form or capable of being printed.

If you have a centralized document destruction program and a company that provides this service, do NOT allow that company to remove documents and destroy them off site. This totally defeats the purpose of classification, document, and access control. If there is any centralized document destruction it must take place under the direct supervision and control of trusted company information protection staff. This includes the removal process and the actual destruction. All destruction must take place on-site and under the direct control and supervision of trusted staff.

Too often staff hold documents in a box on or under their desk until they have a sufficient amount to take it to the document destruction container. It is essential that any document destruction container be locked (with a security lock) and be configured much like a mailbox so that once a paper or document is placed in the container, no one can get in and pull a document out of it. Spies know that if someone took the time to place a document or paper in a destruction bin, it probably was sensitive so these containers are magnets for business spies.

I highly recommend you drive home how important protecting and segregating sensitive information is by having security personnel check on desks and trash. Spot checks can be valuable at identifying and correcting problems. When doing the vulnerability portion of a risk assessment I often look at the "unclassified" general trash to see if there is anything potentially sensitive in the company's regular trash containers. Seventy-five percent of the time I have been able to find sticky notes, printouts, or sensitive information in the regular trash. This is why business spies do trash covers and go through general trash. There are almost always "nuggets" of information carelessly discarded. I even did security test trash covers in the Air Force and, sadly, often found classified information in the general trash.

I have also conducted dozens of trash covers on behalf of companies. I will not do a trash cover unless I am in control of the reporting and can make certain I am not conducting business espionage when doing the trash cover for someone. I ensure that the business I am doing the trash cover for has a legitimate and legal reason for it. In these dozens of trash covers I have done, I have always been successful (over a reasonable time frame) in finding documents that, for example, demonstrate that a company has sensitive business information that originated with a victim company. I find it incredibly ironic that the very company that stole these business secrets originally is not protecting the stolen information and, instead of shredding or controlling destruction, allows the information to be uncovered in a regular trash cover.

Control of Office Machines

Since so many sensitive documents are printed on printers or copy machines, it is important to protect these from abuse or compromise. Since most office machines today have digital memory storage, it is important to prevent individuals from accessing them. This includes not allowing random remote access to the fax machine or copier via phone or computer lines, but also no individual should be permitted to remove the memory storage device without making certain there is no sensitive information stored on the device. It is also especially important to know how equipment is maintained. If it is a fax machine or printer, can it be remotely serviced? If it can, then information can be remotely downloaded. What about the service provider? Maintenance or repair of office machines must be closely monitored by knowledgeable staff if there is a chance there is sensitive business information on them.

Pro-Active Prevention Monitoring

One of the things that always amazes me is that employees can come into the office at odd hours, run up a huge printer/copier tab, download extensively, or email unusual addresses all kinds of sensitive documents and no one seems to know or care.

If security and management would use the tools often already at their disposal and monitor activities based on known *modus operandi* of business spies, they might often see an early "red flag" and reduce the damage and losses significantly. Even past spies have acknowledged that if someone was monitoring these activities it would have at least caused them to have second thoughts or take a totally different route (which, in many cases, would have meant substantially less loss).

Businesses should be encouraged to keep a record of which individuals are making how many copies and for what reason. Many businesses do this already but security doesn't always look at the data, since most look at it as an accounting and financial issue. But printing excessively can also be a security issue. Security can work with management to determine if there is a reason for this. Perhaps a major proposal is being drafted, but then again what if there is no logical explanation? If one individual is making 20 times the number of copies that his/her colleagues are using, this is worth investigating. Instead of just letting the access control records and CCTV recordings be stored on the hard drive and using them for after-the-fact investigations—look at the records in a pro-active and preventive manner. Why is employee Y coming in on weekends at night? Why is he entering zone Z when there does not appear to be any business reason for it? Why is employee A taking a box out at night? Yes. The majority of the time there will be a legitimate reason for this "unusual" behavior but sometimes it will be an indicator of business-espionage-related activities. This tip could become the catalyst for an investigation that will uncover, and thus end, business spying against your company.

Use of Tiger and Red Team Testing

In fact, one of the most important things a company can do to ensure it is maintaining a good counterespionage approach is to constantly monitor and test the components that make up the program. For some reason this is where companies are often the weakest. They may spout the euphemistic phrase of "continuous improvement" and "we must protect our information" but very few companies actually mean it when it comes to security. Security is, in fact, one of the areas where testing can help to determine a program's effectiveness. When there are failures on tests, there is opportunity to enhance or improve security measures.

In one of our tests, it took the penetrating agent 20 minutes and repeatedly stopping employees and even security personnel to try to "turn himself in" and close the test. This is after he penetrated sensitive areas by simply wearing a lab coat and piggybacking. This is after he took multiple sensitive documents laying out unprotected and photographed the manufacturing process. The initial reaction of corporate security was one of shock and outrage. When they found out the penetrating agent used a lab coat that he bought at a local medical supply warehouse they were enraged and claimed the test was "unfair" because their security was designed to stop people wearing street clothing. After some serious discussions about the realism involved in the test, corporate security reluctantly agreed that the test had shown them a vulnerability they had not considered. They were able to make changes and enhance their access control.

I have personally managed to walk through dozens of offices and talked with dozens of people after either sneaking in or piggybacking an employee. I took pictures and picked up documents. Most of the time I was never even questioned or challenged by any employee or security staff. In one instance, I was invited to an office party in the conference room. Yet another time, when walking out the front gate of a facility after getting inside by crawling, undetected, under the fence, I was challenged by a security officer. I thought to myself, better late than never. The officer told me that there were reports of a suspicious individual wandering around the facility and taking pictures. I told the officer I had seen someone dressed in all black and that I had wondered about that person too. I then told the officer I was going for midnight chow (it was 1 a.m.). and when I got back I would let him know if I saw this individual again. The security officer thanked me and let me walk out with my camera and a backpack full of documents and materials.

Yes...penetration tests, in fact tests of all kinds, can be of great value. They can let you know what is working and what is not working. In the latter case, testing allows you to make changes and improve your protection programs. It also gives you a measurable metric for establishing whether your counterespionage program is working or not, and drives home the point that company management takes protecting its business information very seriously.

In fact, in one instance we were told the company culture would not result in employees joining with security to enhance access control. Employees just did not care according to both security and human resources staff. We helped them design a competitive test that involved how long it took each division in the company to identify and report an unauthorized intruder. After two tests, the entire office was on guard, and two weeks later security caught a known building thief after he was identified by staff who thought the intruder was one of the tests. In this case the testing program resulted in employees identifying a real intruder. This is how a program such as this can enhance your physical security.

Non-Disclosure, Non-Compete, and Other Legal Agreements

One of the defenders of intellectual property and trade secrets is clearly the legal department and they have some valuable tools at their disposal. Even though the effectiveness of such legal documents varies from jurisdiction to jurisdiction and from situation to situation, you have potential legal recourse if an individual violates a company's trust, policies, and procedures relating to protected information.

One of the more important documents that can be required of any employee given sensitive information is a non-disclosure agreement. This document is especially worthwhile because it allows the company to specifically identify the kind of information being addressed, the manners by which this information is to be protected, and the consequences if the agreement is not adhered to. Non-compete agreements are also of potential value but each jurisdiction has some unique rules that your legal counsel will have to examine. One issue is whether the employee resigns or voluntarily leaves, is terminated for cause, or was laid off. In the latter case, you might obviously have less latitude. But the non-compete is a potential legal tool that could be used when an employee or someone with authorized access to your sensitive business information abuses that access. Another legal document that could be of value in dealing with business spying is a signed requirement that any technical papers, publications, or presentations that involve a company's sensitive information need to be approved by the company, in writing, before the information can be used. As we know from our case studies, there can be willful and accidental compromises of sensitive business secrets in these situations and this provides the company with an opportunity to discuss the situation and perhaps prevent an accidental or deter a willful compromise.

All business partners should also be required to protect your legitimate sensitive business information. Confidentiality clauses should be placed in all business contracts. This includes those involved in development, manufacturing, parts production, and even service providers.

Of course, none of these legal steps will absolutely prevent business spying or losses of sensitive information such as trade secrets, but having these legal agreements in place can provide you with one more defensive weapon. These tools also help to deter and show others the company is serious about protecting its business secrets. Using these tools can also help define trade secrets and other sensitive and controlled business information in the processing of creating them.

Limiting Where/How Company Information Can Be Worked On or Discussed

It is important that there be some restrictions on where sensitive and protected company information can be discussed and worked on. In most cases classified sensitive information should not be worked on in a forum or venue where unauthorized persons might be able to overhear or oversee that sensitive business information.

These protective restrictions should be specifically covered, with examples, in legal employment documents, company security policies/procedures, and in security education/awareness training. There should be no question in an employee's mind that there is no excuse for working on sensitive information in a public venue where it can be overheard or overseen. This includes talking business secrets on a phone in places like restaurants, bars, hotel lobbies, airplanes, airport lounges, or in chauffeured vehicles or taxis. The list could go on and on, but the important thing is to get people thinking about how easy it is to overhear or to see something on a paper or computer screen when you are, for example, sitting right beside someone.

Since I travel a lot, I see a lot of things on computer screens in airplane seats or lounges. I also overhear some incredibly sensitive information being discussed on phones. While I can only hear one side of the conversation most of the time, what is sometimes loudly blurted out is shocking. It is clear that people are not thinking about the threat. My staff and bosses do not even mention me working a company report or document while on an airplane, because they know the risk. Clearly it is important to make certain employees understand business-spying threats through good education and awareness training and to ensure they are sensitive to all the different environments or ways that information could be accidently compromised. It is also important to discuss home offices, business centers, hotel lobbies, and many other venues where it might not be appropriate to work on or discuss sensitive business information. There are even some places in the office where it might not be appropriate. For example, in smaller offices visitors can often overhear conversations in cubicles within hearing distance from the chairs or couches where they wait. Another example is visitors and cleaning/maintenance/security staff walking through areas where whiteboards and computers are clearly visible to these people who do not need to know such information. After a secondary barrier of sound baffling was added to an office I consulted with, a newspaper reporter was waiting in the reception area and, as he was escorted back to executive offices, made the comment that the company's security was like that of a secret government agency. Since the security measures were based on my recommendations, I took it as a compliment.

Develop Special Measures for Marketing and Sales Staff

Some of the most vulnerable parts of any company, when it comes to business espionage, are members of the sales and marketing staff, since they are all about getting the word out about products and/or services and are very knowledgeable about what's going on within the company. This staff is also very vulnerable because even a novice in social engineering can manipulate most sales and marketing staff into providing some sensitive business espionage information. All you have to do is appear to be an interested potential customer with money to spend and the sales/marketing teams will be doing their best to win you over and that is an ideal way to elicit information.

Because sales and marketing people are all about getting information out to potential clients and the world, they are not the best at keeping business secrets. Some may give up key details, scheduling information, product and manufacturing specifications, and new products/services in development. But if they receive training on the threats to their profession, the *modus operandi* used against marketing/sales staff, and they see that senior management in the company expect them to protect their business secrets, this can be changed. It is important that the sales and marketing staff of a company are actively involved in protecting sensitive company information and resources.

Create a Company Security Culture

One of the most frequent things I hear is that the company culture is just not conducive to effective security. When I hear that I cannot help but wonder if that company "culture" will mean the company will not be around in another 10 years, when all of their business secrets are gone.

Company cultures can be developed and refined by company leaders. Is there sometimes an ethnic/country or regional influence? Of course, but even that can be taken on and changed if leadership charters the course and if employees understand "why." It may not be instantaneous but a company culture can be changed and refined to make it more security conscious.

I have lived and worked in 12 different countries, worked in 63 countries, and in all 50 states in the United States. Every place I go I find there are cultural differences. Having been a consultant in many hundreds of companies all around the world, I am very sensitive to existing cultures, but when threats emerge and people give up implementing important countermeasures because the culture "won't accept it," this is a sign of bad leadership.

For example, I was talking with a company in Asia about a lack of security culture. The senior management told me it would just never happen because the employees did not like security. I had noticed that the company had an amazing culture of safety. Employees were wearing hardhats, safety glasses, reflective vests, and proper footwear. I mentioned that this was also not "cultural" for the environment. The leaders said they were forced to implement it by their corporate headquarters and it had been very difficult for them. I told them it was obvious that they had come a long way toward changing to a good safety culture, and they just needed to take a similar approach for security. They groaned.

Another company told me that their employees would not support security standards and would not report security issues because of their culture. I suggested we get representative employees involved in developing the standards and even the penalties. The company leadership told me it would not work, but finally gave in, while warning me it was a waste of time. The first half of the first day was slow, but once employees understood the potential adverse impact on themselves and their colleagues, they began to participate and soon we had standards and penalties that exceeded those in the home country of the company. We got there because we guided the employees to overcome their cultural barriers. It can be done but I'll admit it is often not easy.

If employees understand the real threats out there and how those threats can adversely impact them and their job and pay, they tend to be more receptive. A lot of it depends on how it is presented. If it appears that the security measures are being implemented because the company does not trust its employees, it may not get a very favorable response by employees, but if employees believe the security measures are designed to protect them from any suspicion, as well as protect their job and both their, and the company's future, they are much more likely to be supportive.

I recommended that a company consider CCTV coverage that would monitor people working with a very sensitive, critical resource. Company leadership told me employees would never tolerate that kind of monitoring. When there was an incident and it appeared a compromise had occurred at the site, we were forced to ask some hard questions of employees. Employees became quite upset, but they also agreed that the circumstances left the company little choice but to draw the conclusion that something happened in their area. I mentioned that if we had CCTV coverage monitoring them they could have been cleared immediately. The innocent ones went, in mass, to leadership and demanded a CCTV camera be installed immediately or they threatened to resign. The key was to stress that the camera would provide exculpatory protection. That changed the culture from one of resenting CCTV monitoring to one that demanded it.

This is an important change that starts at the top. It is important that a company develops and maintains a culture of security. If a company actually has a culture that encourages good security measures, that company will not be a lucrative target for business spying. This is the culture I want to encourage you to develop and nurture.

Liaise with Counterespionage Government Agencies

It is important to be aware of the latest business espionage threats and sometimes government agencies that specialize in countering hostile intelligence services to help you better understand the threats present in a particular location. Generally speaking, many private company security elements are reluctant to work too closely with a government agency for fear that a possible compromise can end up on the nightly news and damage the company's reputation. The other concern is that government agencies want companies to share with them, but they are less than willing to share information with private companies. All of these are valid concerns of some government counterespionage agencies, but I have found that these government agencies can also be good partners, depending the staff you deal with within the agency. With that in mind, it is good to meet with personnel and evaluate the agency as a whole. The potential benefits can be worth the effort.

Offensive Counterespionage

While most of the countermeasures covered thus far have been what I would term "defensive" in nature, there may be a time when "offensive" counterespionage countermeasures are warranted. A company should not automatically rule out such an approach. An "offensive" counterespionage program is activated when it becomes apparent that a business espionage operation is underway and the spying entity is using known business espionage techniques. If an electronic eavesdropping device is used or a driver or cleaning staff member is eavesdropping on conversations, then it is possible to consider passing incorrect information through that spying source. If a competitor or government is conducting a trash cover, throw a document into the trash that is false and misleading, one that could tie up the spies and/or mislead them. If a competitor is trying to hire away or recruit an in-place spy and their method is detected, consider allowing them to "recruit" an internal spy and pass them incorrect information. If a traveler's room is bugged, consider a staged telephone call or staged discussion to mislead whoever is doing the monitoring.

This technique has worked for me on multiple occasions, and has been especially effective when someone is trying to get pricing or bidding information. It also has been used when a particular manufacturing technique does not work but documents and information are passed that causes the competitor to go down an expensive dead-end road before they discover they have been tricked. Such pro-active, offensive countermeasures can cause business spies to question every bit of information they get and often causes them to withdraw and become very circumspect in targeting a particular company for business spying.

Summary

The threat of business espionage is so widespread and has such serious potential consequences that it is worth dedicating some security resources to protecting a company's most sensitive business information from compromise.

It is important to understand that good, basic physical and personnel security measures that can protect you and your employees from theft and robbery, workplace violence, or any number of other security threats also play an important role in the dealing with business espionage threat. But from the recommendations in this chapter it should be clear that all physical and personnel security countermeasures are linked to the business-spying threat and the *modus operandi* used by business spies, which means that traditional security measures need to be expanded and adjusted to incorporate the lessons learned.

If you implement some of these recommended countermeasures you can dramatically lower your vulnerability and, thus, risk exposure to business espionage. This, in turn, can then strengthen the business and make investments in research and development and new strategies more valuable and worthwhile.

10

TECHNICAL ELECTRONIC AND COMPUTER COUNTERMEASURES

Abstract

This chapter addresses countermeasures that can be taken by an organization to deal with the threats that come from technical electronic as well as IT/computer related business spying threats and methods. It includes specific measures in each category that can thwart business spies when they attempt to use these techniques to spy.

Business Espionage
© 2015 Elsevier Inc. All rights reserved.

Introduction

If you accept my premise that the answer to countering business-spying threats is very similar to that for countering other security threats, then the countermeasures approach to both technical electronic and computer spying is to develop strong risk-based, overlapping, and comprehensive countermeasures to those threats. From our case studies (see Chapters 3, 4, 5, and 6) it should be obvious that some of the more significant threats that warrant countermeasures would be the technical electronic threats, such as eavesdropping, and the computer, or cyber-related threats.

First and foremost, it is essential to understand that all threats can evolve but the technical and computer threats are probably changing faster than some of the other security threats. This is especially true in terms of changes in the *modus operandi* used by business spies in the technical electronic and computer fields. All one has to do is look at the changes that are taking place in computer technology and miniaturization, where technological improvements have allowed electronic spying devices in the form of cameras, recorders, and transmitters to be increasingly small, and it is clear why technical and computer threats are so dynamic.

On the technical electronic front, the volume of commercially available concealable cameras, recorders, and transmitters has skyrocketed in the past 20 years. When I started my counterespionage career in the military, espionage devices such as roll-over cameras and concealable microphones were only available to government intelligence and law enforcement. Now high technology espionage devices can be purchased in stores and online. In the spring of 2014, I did a walkthrough of the electronics shops in the Tsim Sha Tsui area of Hong Kong, which is famous for its electronic shops. In two days of combing through the streets and alleys I found some 74 shops selling various types of electronic devices that could readily be used for business spying. On the Internet there are references to hundreds of stores and chains that specialize in spying devices with names like The Spy Store, Spy Shop International, Spy Shop USA, Cheaters Spy Shop, Spy Center, SpyTek, ICU Spy Shop, The Spy Guy, Eye Spy Supply, Spyville, Spy Bubble, and Mobile Spy. Even the widely distributed airline shopping catalog, *Skymall*, regularly advertises between nearly a dozen devices that can be used in business espionage.

Thirty years ago the Internet was just starting and computers were still not that widely deployed in business. Yes, they were used in select industries and for special functions, but the proliferation of computer and mobile devices now cuts across every geographic region and every business sector. Considerable amounts of sensitive information and data are now on computer systems, which have made them literally like bank vaults of information. In fact, I am reminded of the infamous question a reporter asked of bank robber Willie Sutton when he was being hauled off to jail: "Why do you rob banks?" Sutton's answer was so logical it has resonated throughout history: "Because that's where the money is!"[1] Why are computers so important when it comes to business espionage? The answer is similar: Because that's (often) where the sensitive information is!

When it comes to business spying by computer, the key to remember is that it is often via a remote connection by another computer. Remote control of a computer is a big problem because not only is someone spying on you, but this method of spying leaves certain ports, or "backdoors," open. This causes system damage and allows other computer viruses to install themselves, without your knowledge, of course, via backdoors.

Still, the important thing to remember regarding both threats (technical electronic and computer-related) is to first try to prevent and deter, and if that fails to detect early and respond appropriately. In this chapter, we will first discuss some important countermeasures that have helped companies deal with technical electronic threats, and then we'll introduce some countermeasures that work against them.

Technical Surveillance Countermeasures (TSCM)

The approach for dealing with the technical (electronic) penetrations centers around a robust countermeasures program known as a Technical Surveillance Countermeasures, or TSCM, that allows for early detection of spying devices. While discussing the importance of this program, it is necessary to say right upfront that the TSCM business environment is a very specialized arena and is definitely one where experience counts. Yes, it can be expensive to hire or contract a TSCM expert, but do not kid yourself: trying to do a thorough in-house TSCM program will be difficult if you do not have someone who already has at least a decade or more of experience in the

---

[1] Joshua M. Brown, "The Arrest of Willie Sutton," *The Reformed Broker*, February 18, 2012, http://www.thereformedbroker.com/2012/02/18/the-arrest-of-willie-sutton.

profession. Expensive as equipment is, equipment is only part of the program. You have to have someone who knows how to interpret the data the equipment displays. It will also be expensive to the keep up-to-date equipment required as technology evolves. But having TSCM equipment that is up-to-date and able to deal with the latest threat is essential if you want to protect your business secrets from technical/electronic business-related spying.

Limit Access to Sensitive Areas

One of the building blocks for protecting your information from technical compromise is to limit access to areas where sensitive information is displayed or discussed. Listening devices, cameras, and other technical penetrations can come in all forms and anyone who has access has the potential for introducing a device. A simple calculation of the odds tells you that the more exposure there is to various people, the higher the chance of having a bug or listening device left behind. People can also wear recorders, transmitters, and cameras. If you are verbally discussing sensitive information, have it lying out, or displayed on white boards or computer screens, you should known that any visitor or unauthorized individual that gains access to the area has the potential to use it.

It is worth noting that while your primary concern may be an outsider—a competitor or agent of a competitor, a government agency, or a professional spy—the individual planting a device could also be someone with authorized access. In fact, numerically, the number of technical devices I have been able to find most often involved employees or former employees. The latter usually having authorized access at the time they installed or planted the device. The only way to keep the odds down is to limit even employees who have access to areas where sensitive information is discussed or displayed. This includes contractors such as maintenance personnel, cleaning staff, or security staff.

Implement a Formal TSCM Program

One approach to limiting your vulnerability to a technical penetration is to develop and implement a formal TSCM program. So, what does that involve? First and foremost, formally review where and how sensitive information is discussed or displayed. One of the most important concepts is to recognize that the more areas where sensitive information is displayed and discussed, the more the opportunity for compromise and loss there is. Identify where the discussion and display is occurring and then determine if it means there are too many places and restrictions are needed. Typical locations where sensitive data is discussed or displayed include executive offices, conference rooms, purchasing and contracting areas, operations areas, server rooms, research and development areas, or laboratories. Locations might also include special events such as board meetings, sales meetings, and events where sensitive information will be discussed. Analyze your business and processes and determine where these areas are. Make modifications if you can limit the locations where sensitive information is displayed. Focus first and foremost on the most critically sensitive information. Next, you must "harden" those areas by limiting access and controlling the area. Anyone without a need-to-know—and that includes cleaning people, maintenance staff, and contract security personnel—should not be given routine, unescorted access to areas where sensitive information is discussed or displayed.

Consider a regular (but not fixed and predictable) scheduled TSCM sweep to try and determine if there are any surreptitious devices being used in any of the identified locations where sensitive information is discussed or displayed. Depending on the amount of sensitive information and the criticality of that information to your business (business impact), you might determine a quarterly sweep is needed. It may only be an annual sweep. Then think about the special events where having an on-site sweep could be of value. The longer the time frame between sweeps and the sheer number of individuals that have regular access to the area are both important factors for determining the frequency of sweeps. If you sweep a hotel conference room for a special event but then do not control access to the area you have potentially wasted your money and effort. Once a sweep is complete, it is only as valid as your access controls and the time passed. As time passes and more individuals access the area, the higher the potential becomes that someone has planted a listening device or camera since you conducted the sweep. Once it is understood that a regular TSCM sweep is an important countermeasure, the question I am regularly asked is, "How do you select a good TSCM service provider?"

Like so many other things, it has to do with the expertise, experience, and professionalism of the provider. Here are some things to examine and think about when making that decision:
- How much experience does the individual doing the sweep have? Where did the individual doing the sweep learn how to do a TSCM sweep and how many years has he or she been conducting sweeps?

- What kind of equipment will the provider be employing? Here is a list of some of the key pieces of equipment that a good TSCM specialist would employ:

    Digital telephone analyzer (focuses on digital telephone compromises)

    RF spectrum analyzer (looks for surveillance devices transmitting via radio frequencies)

    Broadband radio frequency analyzer (looks for surveillance devices transmitting via broadband radio frequencies)

    Telephone line analyzer (looks for any unexpected feeds off internal telephone lines)

    Non-linear junction detector (areas are examined using a non-destructive radar that can spot semi-conductor electronic components such as transistors and diodes, which are the building blocks of electronic surveillance devices)

    Infrared/thermal detector (looks for heat that is emitted by spycams, bugs, and electronic circuits even if devices are inside furniture, walls, or ceiling tiles)

    Laser refractor (looks for defused laser signals that can come from someone trying to use lasers to listen to conversations from windows and glass vibrations or from some cameras)

    Other telephone line and instrument detectors (as simple as determining if a given wire is transmitting an electric signal to more sophisticated signal testing devices)

Ask for a sample sweep report so you can see how thorough and comprehensive the typical report is. A report should include, at minimum:

- The who, what, when, where, and how of the sweep
- A listing of what equipment was used in the sweep
- A detailed listing of the equipment and areas swept
- The results of each of the equipment and areas swept
- Any "findings" or concerns
- A list of references you can contact
- Proper licensing as a security firm or private investigator in your state/jurisdiction; proper business registration and insurance coverage
- A listing of professional affiliations; at minimum they should include some of the following:

    ASIS International

    Business Espionage Controls and Countermeasures Association (BECCA)

    Espionage Research Institute International (ERII)

    Information Systems Audit and Control Association

Another frequently asked question I hear is, "What will I need to do if I want to get a quote for a TSCM sweep and prepare for the sweep?" After you select a provider, you will need to give that provider the full address, the various sensitive projects that occur in the area to be assessed (preferably broken down by office or location within the facility), the date you want the sweep to occur, the area in square feet or meters, and the key functional locations within the complex. You will have to have the keys or master key ready to give the examiner the opportunity to get in all offices, rooms, and closets. You will have to limit the individuals who know about the sweep to the absolute minimum and any considerations of doing a sweep and the actual conduct of a sweep should not be discussed in the sweep area. I hope it is obvious that if those who have planted the electronic bugs know you are going to do a TSCM sweep, they will have an opportunity to deactivate or remove devices before the sweep if they get advanced warning. Additionally, you will need to decide what your company wants to do should a technical spy device be discovered. It goes without saying, I hope, that a fundamental principle here is, once again, to limit who will know there was a "find." The options to consider if there are finds include:

- Remove and deactivate after documenting the presence
- Leave the device(s) in place and limit access to the area
- Try to determine who planted it and who is monitoring the device(s)
- Consider reporting the discovery to appropriate law enforcement agencies
- Continue with normal business activities
- Pass deceptive information

Other Locations Where You Can Be Victimized by Technical Spying

The business locations mentioned in the chapter on business impact/consequences are important, and that is why it is wise to focus a TSCM program that includes sweeps of all of those locations. This includes the offices of senior executives, finance, marketing, human resources, research and development, legal, conference/meeting rooms, and IT/server rooms. But you may not be able to limit your technical spying vulnerability to the office building or complex. There are potentially other locations where you may be discussing sensitive information and have sensitive information that can be viewed. These could include:

- Hotel rooms or hotel conference rooms, even hotel lobby areas
- Chauffeured vehicles, taxis, or personal vehicles
- Aircraft (chartered or commercial)
- Airport lounges
- Trade show venues
- Restaurants, bars, or coffee shops
- Homes and home offices

There are at least three groups that can be extracted from the list above and that means there are at least three approaches to take, as each of the groups depends on the venue. If it is a vehicle, aircraft, or conference room that you control, you can extend the TSCM sweep program to include those venues and you can use some good access controls. If it is one you do not control—a rental vehicle or limousine service, commercial aircraft, hotel lobby, restaurant, bar, etc.—the best approach is education/awareness/policy/procedure and discipline so employees do not discuss sensitive information at these uncontrolled venues. If it is a hotel room or hotel conference room, you can consider a sweep and then restrict access until you depart but you have to be able to exercise positive control over those venues until you leave. The authority to do this should be part of the agreement you sign with the hotel or location you choose for a conference. If it is a chartered aircraft, a personal vehicle, or home office, you should be able to do sweeps and maintain some reasonably restrictive access controls over a longer period of time but as soon as you have people coming inside to do repairs, cleaning, etc., you have expanded the potential that a post-sweep device has been introduced.

Prevention and Early Detection

While detection of potential penetrations is important, the best TSCM countermeasures should focus on prevention. This goes back to education and awareness of security forces, management, and employees. All visitors should be required to declare if they have any items on them that record, take photos, or transmit. All of those devices should have to be turned off and the battery removed before they are given access to areas where sensitive information is available. If a visitor is acting in an unusual manner and appears to be holding stilted conversations or standing with an unusual posture or position, these are signs the individual could be trying to covertly record, transmit, or copy.

In addition to physical access controls, it would also be good to have sound baffling for walls and vents, white-noise generators running, and heavy acoustic curtains up to deflect sounds on windows and walls.

Computer countermeasures

Given the amount of information now manipulated and stored on computers and computer systems, it is important to have good IT and computer security countermeasures in place. What are some things that should be considered when looking at potential countermeasures to the threat of computer-related business espionage? Many of the best things you can do—no great surprise here—are the same things that IT security experts have been recommending for at least a decade:

- Keep your software up-to-date and the latest security repairs installed
- Install a firewall
- Install the latest anti-spyware and anti-virus software
- Have a back-up capability for all stored information and consider off-line data storage for your most sensitive information (limiting the value of Internet-connected hacking)
- Require and use complex passwords that involve a mixture of letters, numbers, and symbols and are at least 10 or more characters in length (they should be changed periodically, probably at least every 90 days)
- Use automatic time-out settings and a password-protected screensaver when the computer has not been used after a period of time (usually one minute is the best practice standard)
- Have uninterrupted power supply (UPS) capability and employ surge protection.
- Through education and awareness training warn employees of the dangers of downloading emails and attachments from unknown sources or third-party sites
- Consider encryption so someone with unauthorized access to a computer or mobile device cannot easily gain access to emails and documents
- When you have staff traveling, know the highest threats (see Chapter 3) and consider requiring travelers to only use a "dumb" phone/smartphone and a sterile laptop that has no sensitive information stored on them

Audit Logs

One very important security feature of server systems is an audit program. Audit programs are used to record the activities of system users. Things like failed log-ons and attempts to access restricted files can be very important. Unusual usage times and large downloads should also draw security's attention. It is also important to protect these logs from compromise for after-the-fact investigation. This means you need mirrored logs where every time the audit program has a log entry, an identical entry is created on that separate, mirrored log and a separate computer/hard-drive. If security or system administrators regularly look at what is happening on the system, it can allow intervention before some of the most sensitive information is lost to spies. The key is that the person reviewing needs to be up-to-date on the latest *modus operandi* of business spies and be matching these red flags against actual trends in use.

Specific intrusion detection software can be especially valuable. Since hackers and intruders are constantly trying to exploit vulnerabilities and get into IT systems it is important to detect attempted breaches early and to respond. Sometimes it is even possible to catch the individuals conducting the attack. Although it is expensive and time consuming to install intrusion and abuse detection software on all systems, it is important for those housing sensitive and proprietary information. There are a number of excellent commercially available intrusion and abuse detection tools available. You can even install a basic tool called Tripwire for free from the Internet. Having this early detection capability is an important tool to preventing business spying.[2]

Write-Protected Disks

In many cases, hackers have attempted to increase the value of the information they stole by not only stealing the sensitive information, but also by covering their tracks with file destruction. By using write-protected disks you will have this back-up information available should someone want to cover their tracks or do damage to your information on your servers.

Intrusion Detection Software

It is also worth having the latest software that will allow you to get an early warning of a breach of your IT system. This software can alert security so they can cut a successful penetration off quickly and limit the damage. It can also provide an early warning that someone is targeting the system.

[2] Ira Winkler, *Corporate Espionage*, Prima Publishing, 1997.

User Education and Awareness Training

It should come as no surprise that one of the most common vulnerabilities is, in my experience, email with the concealed Trojan horse software, usually in the form of a download. This can come from an email or a thumbdrive, which illustrates the point that the most important and effective countermeasures revolve around the user. If users are educated and aware of the threats, understand and avoid falling into the traps laid out in the *modus operandi* of the business spies, and report potential espionage attempts, this combination forms the ideal means of early business-spying discovery and ultimate defeat of the spies.

Download Warning

Closely linked to the security education and awareness component is a technique employed by some companies where anytime a user is going to download an attachment from an email or inserts a thumbdrive to download a document, a detailed warning comes us and requires a specific action on the part of the user to guarantee the user is knowledgeable of the sender/source, the legitimacy of the download, the vital importance of the download, and how the user can double check it with virus and other protective software. Since so many computer attacks start this way, it is important that this process be considered. Of course, one option is to keep certain sensitive information on segregated servers and not allow most users the privilege of downloading from an email or even inserting a thumbdrive into a computer. While this works, it was often too disruptive and many companies don't restrict users in this way, which also results in more compromises. A good example is the alleged Alcoa email breach by five officers of Unit 61398 of the Chinese People's Liberation Army.[3]

Computer Forensics

While not a prevention technique, if you are wondering if someone has gotten access to your computer or mobile device and what they may have downloaded, you may consider contacting a computer forensic specialist who can do an analysis on the computer and hard drive to see what kind of activity has been taking place. This is what we did when a consultant colleague of mine began seeing some strange reactions on a computer taken to

---

[3] Devlin Barret and Siobhan Gorman "Chinese Charged in U.S Hacks," *Wall Street Journal*, May 20, 2014.

Vietnam. A computer forensic specialist did an analysis of the laptop when it returned to its home base and the forensic expert was able to explain which documents on the computer had apparently been accessed and copied. The same thing happened with computers returned by the Chinese police when a supposed migrant worker stole the laptops of research and development specialists, or when a security officer stole removable hard drives in Mexico. In all of these cases, a forensic analysis helped determine that copying of information had taken place so the incidents were not as innocent as might have seemed.

Specific Computer Security Contracts

While it may not seem that important, experience has shown that another critical part of protecting a company from computer-related spying is to have very specific security-related contract terms for any IT-related support or supply contracts or agreements. These contracts should specify that the contractor entity is responsible for security of the systems specified in the contract. According to an *CSO Magazine* article in 2014, both private companies and government entities are notoriously bad at addressing security in IT contracts. "Security is often left out of contract negotiations. ..." the article notes and then concludes that this approach to contracting leaves a major vulnerability for the company since the contractor often fails to fix vulnerabilities if it is not specifically required in the contract.

Summary for Computer Countermeasures

The prevalence of data on computers is just one of the reasons why it is important to use encryption and to have strong physical security and access controls in place. If travel is necessary and the computer owner is not physically in the direct possession of the device 24/7, or if the device is used to access the Internet in many different countries, there is a high probability it will be compromised. Therefore, it is recommended that companies have highly sanitized travel computers so the information on the hard drive is limited to that which can be compromised without a severe adverse business impact.

Given that keystroke readers and other electronic devices that record data based on electronic inputs are involved in some computer information security compromises, it is also important that TSCM sweeps, IT logs, and other record checks are constantly looking for possible physical access penetrations as these devices generally have to be physically connected to the computer system.

So, the bottom line is that technical electronic and computer business spying are regular occurrences and companies must have robust programs in place to prevent or at least detect spying as early as possible. With all the sensitive information available, business spies will be turning to technical electronic eavesdropping and computer spying to try and get that information. You must do your best to neutralize them as quickly as possible.

Mobile Device Countermeasures

There is one threat and potential vulnerability that cuts across both of these categories and it warrants separate mention. In today's business world there is widespread use of mobile/cellular phones and devices. These pose special threats/vulnerabilities and warrant special attention.

After the Edward Snowden disclosures, it is even more clear what we already knew. The U.S. National Security Agency (NSA) monitors such devices. Guess what? So do most of the other government agencies. In fact, it is amazing that senior business executives and even government leaders still use unprotected mobile devices. Part of the Snowden disclosures revealed that the NSA allegedly monitored the mobile device of the German Chancellor, Angela Merkel. If she was using an unprotected device, shame on her. The same is true for any other business or government executive.[4]

There are more than a hundred commercially available cellphone/mobile device-monitoring capabilities readily available on the Internet. This includes components that can be placed inside the device or software that can be loaded, sometimes even remotely. As a result, those monitoring can surreptitiously listen in on and record phone conversations, retrieve voicemails, read emails, or SMS text messages, determine (by GPS) where the phone is geographically located, and even activate the camera and retrieve photographs or video.

In fact, Andy Coulson, a former top newspaper editor, was convicted in the United Kingdom of conspiring to intercept phone voicemails.[5] There are dozens of cases where private investigators have used hacking techniques to obtain evidence of spouses cheating or employees involved in misconduct. Less known is how often it is used in business spying but the potential application is evident. There is also a special vulnerability when users are oblivious to the threat and constantly need to communicate on their mobile device.

---

[4] Jeevan Vasagar, "Berline Arrests Suspected US Agent," *Financial Times Weekend*, July 5-6, 2014.
[5] Alexis Flynn, "Ex-Editor Jailed in Hacking Case," *Wall Street Journal*, July 5-6. 2014.

The countermeasures are challenging because there are so many different mobile devices, all with different vulnerabilities. This is especially true if government agencies are the perpetrators. The main countermeasure is the same as for most business-spying threats: user education and awareness. Knowing that it only takes a phishing download or 5 to 10 minutes of access to the mobile device to load the tracking/monitoring software, it is, therefore, incumbent on the device holder to keep the device on his/her person at all times and not download suspicious or unknown attachments. Likewise, it is important that mobile devices not be allowed to be present during sensitive meetings or conversations. Governments and companies that care about protecting their sensitive information require that all devices be turned off, batteries removed, and devices be stored away from the area where sensitive discussions or meetings are held. Since the devices can be remotely turned on, simply turning off the device is not sufficient protection. Devices that include access to email must use encrypted emails and have password protection to prevent others from easily reading emails and accessing systems.

Summary

This chapter covered countermeasures to two very important threats: technical and computer threats. It is important to understand that these two areas seem to garner the biggest headlines and one could surmise that if you focus on these two threats, you have addressed business spying. While my hat is off, in a salute, to the IT security professionals and to those security professionals who focus on the technical threats, I believe this is a case where the experts on those threats have been doing a better job at educating their workforce than detecting and addressing the threats. These threats are substantial and very important to address but the overall business espionage threat perspective is complicated and usually involves a combination of threat vectors. While legislators in the U.S. and several countries are introducing new laws that could increase the criminal penalties for business spying and also increase the opportunity for legal civil remedies for victims of trade secret theft, that means a company has already suffered the loss and the best course of action is to be pro-active and preventative.[6] Relying only on after-incident reactive legal recourses is not a wise and prudent strategy.

[6] Megan Gates, "License to Steal," *Security Management Magazine*, June, 2014.

COMPREHENSIVE COUNTERMEASURES

Abstract

This chapter is an attempt to avoid the problem of dividing physical/personnel security and technical and IT security into distinct organizational divided silos. While chapters 8 and 9 addressed these threats separately, this chapter explains why each organization much ensure that these two security elements work together, cooperate and function as a team, perhaps under a chief security officers (CSO) function.

Introduction

One of the biggest problems I regularly see in existing programs that attempt to protect a company from business espionage is a lack of coordination between organizational functions that divide security into organizational divisions or silos such as cyber/IT-oriented security and physical security. Other organizational silos that could adversely impact security effectiveness include human resources, contracting, legal, facilities, and even operations. The problem with those organizational divisions is that spies exploit the seams between the various elements to more effectively get to and steal information.

Almost every organization I have tried to help has told me, during initial conversations, that their organization does not have those kinds of problems. For example, they will often tell

Business Espionage
© 2015 Elsevier Inc. All rights reserved.

me that within their organization, IT security and physical security "work closely together." In almost every instance, these departments certainly may have made some efforts to work together, but as I found, turf battles are often so significant that most of the time these groups run largely independently of each other and do not share a great deal of information in a timely and pro-active manner. After all, in turf battles, information can mean power. This is especially disconcerting within the security where both IT and physical security efforts run largely independently and hence less than efficiently and often even ineffectively. One of the most frequent comments heard goes something like (in this example, the comments would be coming from the physical security personnel): "Oh, that would fall under IT security and we need to stay out of that during this assessment. They do their own assessment." That kind of comment is a "red flag" that indicates this will likely be an overall security issue within the organization.

IT security will not be very effective if spies are able to gain physical access to servers and networks. Physical security relies on IT systems to provide communications and security-related records. Physical security will not be very effective if information and communications systems are compromised. The majority of access control and CCTV systems use IT for communications and most of the equipment used to store this data is often found within IT server room or IT "closets." If IT has poor physical security it can undermine the physical security of the entire organization/facility as suddenly access control systems and records or CCTV systems and records are not available.

From our case studies in earlier chapters it should be apparent that most espionage attacks are often multi-pronged and involve both physical security and IT types of security attacks. The targeted information is frequently maintained on IT systems, but the ability to get to that information is not limited to traditional IT-only attacks, especially external only attacks. Instead, spies tend to look at physical security vulnerabilities and exploit those first. With the information or access gained by physical compromises (e.g., by social engineering and insiders), spies are then able to exploit IT vulnerabilities that occur when someone has legitimate internal, and maybe even physical, access to equipment.

A few years ago (approximately 2012) I was doing a risk assessment with the objective of being the protection of a company's most valuable and sensitive information inside China. As I worked with the separate silos of IT and physical security, it was apparent that both had recently been under attack, and both were trying to harden their defenses after the attacks. As I worked on the timeline it appeared that the spies had first attempted to attack the IT systems directly by hacking in from outside. When simple hacking failed, they began to do what most spies resort to—they tried to get individuals to gain access by pretending that they were a service vendor to try and get physical access to the server room and IT systems. They also attempted to pay some of the existing employees to give them access to the company's IT systems. To their credit, some employees reported this to security. While physical security had noted that there were people apparently trying to gain physical access to the company's offices, they did not specifically alert IT. IT, on the other hand, had thwarted efforts to hack into their system remotely but they failed to advise physical security that there had been apparent attacks. If the first element attacked (IT) had notified its counterparts, the physical security element might have been better prepared to deal with the next attack. This is the value of breaking down organizational silos and working closely together. It is often the difference between effective and ineffective security and sensitive information protection.

For example, when eight men were arrested for tapping into a Barclay's bank branch in London in 2013, it was learned that one of the gang posed as an engineer and was able to use that pretext to get into the server room, a breach of physical security within an IT-controlled area. The individual who was able to talk his way into the server room installed a keyboard video mouse (KVM) on the system and that allowed the information gatherers (spies) to pick up keystrokes/passwords and then remotely access accounts. IT security was compromised but it was compromised after physical security was circumvented and compromised by a spy who persuaded someone, using social engineering, that he should be given unauthorized and unmonitored access to the bank's server room. Improved physical security that addressed social engineering threats could have prevented an IT security compromise.

In approximately 2013, I was working with a company with poor physical security in their server room. The door and lock could be easily compromised and there was also a large glass window that offered potential undetected access into the server room. Because the IT personnel did not want the hassle of turning on and off alarms, there was no intrusion detection system protecting the server room and the only CCTV camera was oriented to cover someone entering through the main door. In addition to those vulnerabilities, cleaning staff, who were rotating contract employees, were given unrestricted and unsupervised access to the server area several times a day. While the company minimized the importance of working together with an integrated IT/physical security approach, barely a year later a Russian engineer who no longer worked with the company (former employee) was identified when stealing the company's latest trade secrets. When he was arrested, he admitted that after he left, he had compromised multiple current employees with legitimate access to the information, and some contract employees who had indirect access, and had them download/gather volumes of sensitive information, or he used legitimate credentials to access information he then passed to the competition for money. Had physical security been better and had they communicated to IT security, the compromises could have been detected early and potentially stopped. If IT had pro-actively detected possible excessive and unauthorized copying or downloading of sensitive information, physical security could have identified the potential internal culprits and neutralized them early before there were such large-scale compromises.

Formal Integrated Approach to IT and Physical Security

It is important to formalize the process by which IT and physical security entities work together. A chief security officer (CSO) responsible for ensuring the convergence of both IT and physical security can be an important initiative and approach to this. The professional security organization, ASIS International, has long advocated that companies consider a convergent security program and have a CSO that is responsible for both physical and IT/cyber security.[1] One of the better illustrations for this lack of understanding of the business espionage threat is a report prepared every 2 years by Securitas Security Services, Inc. The most recent report was based on a survey of U.S. Fortune 1000 companies in 2012, which listed cyber/communications security as the number one threat facing Fortune 1000 companies.

In fact, the top 10 perceived threats/issues reported were:
- Cyber Security
- Workplace Violence Prevention/Response
- Business Continuity
- Employee Screening

---

[1] "ASIS International Releases CSO American National Standard," *Security Today*, January 6, 2009.

- Property Crime
- Employee Theft
- Crisis Management and Response
- Unethical Business Conduct
- Litigation for Inadequate Security
- Identity Theft[2]

Where did business espionage place in this survey on perceived threats? It was way down the list as number 16 (in basically the same position as the previous survey in 2010). I asked a number of security directors how they made that decision and the answer was usually that business espionage was largely about physical security and IT/cyber security was a different, more prevalent and emerging threat.

While IT/cyber security is a major security issue for companies, and may well warrant the number one ranking, a good part of the reason it is a top threat is because the cyber avenue is so often used for theft of sensitive business information, which is the focus of business espionage. In fact, cyber theft of information can be accurately defined as one method by which business espionage is carried out. If cyber security is the number one issue, business espionage should probably be up in the number two or number three position. But the fact that business espionage is way down at number sixteen is *prima facie* evidence that there is a problem with understanding the business-spying threat and understanding that most IT/cyber theft is a method or technique of committing business espionage. The two are closely interrelated, even if businesses do not comprehend this connection.

A further indication of the issue was reflected in how many major corporations reported they were hurrying to build-up and enhance their cyber security. The *Wall Street Journal* reported that IT security is on the agenda when Kellogg Company's directors meet. Their answer? Kellogg created a security group for IT and hired the company's first chief information officer. That officer, Steven Young, was quoted as saying the company was most concerned about theft of its production processes (i.e., business espionage) and the article goes on to say that Kellogg makes certain its trade secrets about how it makes cereal are stored on machines not connected to the Internet. Other boards, according to the *Wall Street Journal*, reportedly focusing on this threat include Exxon Mobil Corporation, Tyson Foods, Inc., Delta Air Lines Inc., and Wal-Mart.[3]

---

[2] "Top Security Threats and Management Issues Facing Corporate America," Securitas Survey of Fortune 1000 Companies, 2012.
[3] Danny Yadron, "Corporate Boards Race to Shore Up Cybersecurity," *Wall Street Journal*, June 30, 2014.

In fact, the article went on to note that in 2014, 1517 companies traded on the New York Stock Exchange or Nasdaq Stock Market listed cyber security, hacking, hackers, cyber attacks, or data breach as a business "risk" in their security filings.[4]

It is important to understand that cyber-security issues are most frequently linked to espionage. In fact, that is exactly what cyber-security company Symantec said when referring to attacks on utility companies. In the reports the focus was a suspected state-sponsored group of hackers that had been employing various techniques to access corporate computer networks, including injecting malware into third-party software, e-mails, and websites. In this way, the attackers had the capability to launch sabotage campaigns that could have wreaked havoc on energy supplies in several European countries. Symantec explained that Dragonfly had collected system information with the help of Backdoor Oldrea, gaining access to Outlook address books and lists of programs and files found on the compromised computers. The hackers used Trojan.Karagany to upload the information they had stolen, download new files, and run them on infected machines. The majority of companies subjected to the attack were based in the U.S., France, Germany, Italy, Spain, Poland, and Turkey. The operation was discovered by Symantec, which said that "espionage appeared to be the primary motivation for the hackers."[5]

In fact, the security experts and government counterintelligence officials that I regularly talk with have basically stated that between 60 and 80 percent of the IT/cyber attacks that occur are focused on business espionage, which almost exactly mirrors my personal experience with companies around the world.

Clearly much of the business community should learn more about the difference between threat and risk, and also should ensure a better understanding of the threat of business espionage, which includes, but is broader than, just IT/cyber security in isolation. A chief information officer and chief/director of corporate security should probably both report to a corporate security officer, probably at least at a vice president level, so there is a convergence of the two inter-related security functions when it comes to dealing with a major but complex threat such as business espionage.

---

[4] Ibid.
[5] Russell Dickinson, "Over 1100 Energy Companies Fall Victim to Dragonfly Attack," July 27, 2014, https://www.misco.co.uk

Other Integrated Approaches to Security

If IT/cyber and physical security are the only dysfunctional elements when it comes to trying to have effective security for countering business spying within an organization, it might be easier to create a counterespionage program. But there are other functional areas that have also proved to not work closely with the security functions we identified during our case studies. Among those is human resources (HR). In my experience HR often does not work closely enough with physical and IT security. I know of at least three instances where a spy was allowed into an office area by HR under the pretext of seeking a job. The spy then wandered around the building, including sensitive areas, and removed copies of materials, before departing. HR has also all too frequently failed to coordinate resignations/terminations with both security and IT elements in a timely (e.g., advance) manner, which allowed individuals to keep accessing their email and company accounts to download information. Poor physical security, combined with HR's failure to coordinate terminations/separations, has allowed terminated/separated individuals to access office areas after their departure because people let them in without a badge or they were allowed to retain their badge by HR/management and their access was not terminated. When company property is returned, it is also good to coordinate that with IT and physical security. For example, some significant losses could have been prevented if IT security had imaged a terminated/separated employee's computer and checked to see what kind of information they had been downloading prior to leaving. When an individual has access to sensitive company information, it is important to have that recognized and documented during exit interviews, and IT security and corporate security should be checking on any possible loss of sensitive information from any employees leaving the company.

Another major problem that regularly surfaces is the lack of coordination between physical/IT security when it comes to selecting facilities to house operations. Even selection of housing for expatriates internationally has a security component. It is important to have both IT and physical security involved in the selection process to ensure the space selected is located in a relatively safe environment and there are not known competitive threats in the same complex, for example. This means that IT and physical security both work with procurement and facilities and are given a voice in the ultimate location selection process. As a result of going over physical layouts, or specifying required improvements in security, this multi-disciplined team can ensure that the security in the new office or facility is not going to be challenging because of systems issues, layout, or similar facility-related issues.

Contracting/procurement also needs to work closely with security so that information protection issues are addressed in all contracting documents. In my experience, some of the worst compromises occurred when cleaning staff or security staff were or became spies. Similarly, some of the worst physical and IT security I have seen has been within contract security companies or out-sourced law firms and accounting firms. These contracted firms often have a considerable amount of a company's sensitive business information but do not provide good security for the sensitive information they have access to and/or maintain. While a spy might have difficulty getting trade secrets because of layered security measures in place at a high-tech firm's offices, a law firm that has the company's advance patent or trade secret information at an office with a flimsy door/lock, no intrusion detection system, no CCTV, and no locked containers would be an "easy" target. Likewise, a contract security firm that often conducts a risk assessment, or at least a security survey or vulnerability assessment, and identifies all the vulnerabilities at a site, but keeps the report with this potentially damaging information not adequately protected at the security company's main offices, is also an easy target.

Too many security companies have poor physical security and it is easy to find personnel records, financial records, and reports identifying security issues just lying around unprotected. A good test is to visit your security company office and see if they have access control systems and if everyone is wearing a photo identification badge. You want to verify their IT security and ensure they mark and lock up documents related to you business. If not, you might want to look elsewhere for your security partner.

So, which locations would a spy most likely target? The answer is obvious: the ones with the lowest levels of effective security. If a contracted firm is given access, as a course of their duties, to sensitive operational, R & D, legal, security, or financial information they should be required to meet established minimum security standards. They should also be audited to ensure their compliance with those standards. Once again, this requires that security elements, contracting, and facilities all work closely together and that is often easier said than done, but if it is a part of the policies/procedures for contracting/procurement, it is more likely to be accomplished.

This office is very typical of a number of business offices around the world. It could be compacted into a cubicle or expanded slightly with more space and furnishings for a senior executive, but this "typical business office" should now be looked at in a different way after examining all the potential threats from business espionage. Here are just a few of the many counterespionage concerns that a company should have with a typical office space. Is the office area locked? Who has access? Why is there no "clean desk" policy in place? Why are there so many file folders in the desk area? Are they properly marked and caveated? Why are there no locks on the file and desk drawers? Who has the key? Why is there no pulverizing shredder? What about the waste basket where sensitive information could inadvertently find its way? Do all of the pencils/pens come from a secure source? Are there any decorations in the office that were gifts? Have they been checked? Is the computer secured and is there a screensaver and a frequently changed password required? Could an unauthorized person access the system from the desktop? Where is the printer located and how is it serviced? Is the telephone line and hardware secure? Has there been a Technical Surveillance Countermeasures Sweep done recently and did it include the lights and electrical outlets? We look at the threats to an office with a much different way of thinking when we are sensitive to the threats and vulnerabilities from business espionage.

Summary

A comprehensive security approach illustrates why it is so important to tailor business espionage security solutions to a risk-based approach, one that is holistic and encompasses the entire organization. As I hope you can surmise by drawing on the case studies and countermeasures discussed in previous chapters, the fundamental building blocks for this comprehensive program are:
- A thorough and complete risk assessment
- Senior management support

- Solid and detailed security policies and procedures
- A tailored counter espionage security education and awareness program so employees can learn and apply knowledge of threats, countermeasures, and consequences to their specific functional areas and jobs
- Similar requirements for all contract elements that could be considered "insiders"
- Effective IT/cyber security measures
- Effective physical security measures

While there may be some differences in the *modus operandi* spies would typically employ against you if you work in IT or are the administrative assistant to the head of finance, the important thing is early detection of potential efforts to circumvent security protective measures and quick reporting that allows a response that is coordinated throughout the company and that cuts across functional organizational silos/divisions for fast and maximum effectiveness.

CONCLUSION

It is my sincere hope that after reading the case studies and examples of business spying covered in the previous chapters, you now have a better understanding of business espionage threats, vulnerabilities, business impacts, and, hence, the business-espionage-related risks present in the twenty-first century. I believe that the recommended countermeasures can help you deal with the threats and to reduce any identified vulnerabilities.

It should also be clear that in some places in the world there are increased levels of business spying happening, but it should also be clear that business espionage can and does occur almost everywhere. I provided my "dirty dozen" high-threat countries for business spying as a starting point, but spying activities are happening anywhere people do business, and if you have a business, you have a competition, which increases the potential for business spying.

Overview of Business Spying Lessons Learned

When you examine the publicly disclosed business spying incidents and those that have never been publically disclosed but that have been shared with you in this book, you can extract some lessons you can apply to a risk-based security program to counter business spying. The following reflects some of these lessons.

Threat Analysis

As we have learned, threats can come from outsiders (government-conducted espionage, competitors, or competitor-hired spies, professional spies, etc.), but they can also come from within the organization (disgruntled employees, ambitious employees, careless employees, disloyal employees, contractors, etc.). In many situations, threats will involve a combination of outsiders and insiders, as well as multiple techniques.

Business-spying methods/techniques used include:
- Social engineering where those with legitimate access are "talked out" of information or the spies are able to talk or otherwise manipulate their way through employees who give up information or grant access to sensitive areas. This can be in

person, over the telephone, or via the Internet. This is especially relevant at trade shows, conferences, etc., where sales and marketing people are specifically targeted.

- False flag/front companies that are closely linked to social engineering and are sometimes used to mask the true identity of the one making an inquiry. Pretending to be a potential customer is a good way to get information, especially from sales staff and pretending to be an employee of a partner or someone interested in a job can allow manipulation of human resources staff.
- Relatedly, companies enter into partnerships—especially in foreign environments—where their partner exploits the partnership to steal sensitive information and use that theft to launch a competitive product or business. In fact, trusted parties and partners are the most prevalent example of sensitive information theft. Business spying is more than eight times more likely to involve a trusted party/partner than any other form and four times more frequent than all others combined. [1]
- Eavesdropping in bars, restaurants, lobbies/elevators, coffee shops, airports, or on aircraft (what one company that specialized in this for high-tech companies called "listening to the nerds"). This might involve recording devices but usually is just an individual or individual spies working an airliner, hotel, elevator, or restaurant/bar.
- Electronic eavesdropping using concealed cameras, microphones, transmitters in work areas, hotels, and residences that are planted during break-ins, through "legitimate" access as workers, by insiders, or via devices that are temporarily carried into the facility where they can be installed and/or left behind, or worn into the facility by a visitor, worker, etc. Through this means spies can gather sensitive information when the holders of the information are unaware.
- Exploiting use of cellular telephones, cordless telephones, speaker phones, satellite telephones, VoiP, or Bluetooth devices to listen to conversations.
- Using physical access to a computer system/component or use a virus, compromised device, or other means to penetrate and transfer sensitive data from a computer system to an unauthorized user.

---

[1] Katleen Ohlson, "Survey: Fortune 1000 Companies Losing Billions in Stolen Information," CNN, Setpember 28, 1999, www.cnn.com/tech/computing/9909/28/fortune.1jk.idg.

- Stealing or copying of laptop, removable hard drive, or mobile device when left unattended or unprotected, or stolen from an office, hotel, or residence.
- Breaking into or exploiting otherwise legitimate access to, an office, residence, hotel, or vehicle to steal documents, materials, prototypes, or provide access to servers, thumbdrives, or other storage areas/devices left unsecured.
- Through break-in, social engineering, or through remote access, getting a hard drive or access to information maintained on the hard drives of printers, copiers, etc. This can occur in office areas or in residences where devices are kept and used for business purposes.
- Recruiting an existing and targeted employee or employees away from a company to bring the knowledge and information they possess with them; this can include senior leadership or working level staff, including IT, secretarial and administrative staff. This can be accomplished through flattery or money (and combination thereof) offered by recruiters and private investigators.
- Recruiting existing employees to provide information or plant a newly hired employee or contractor (undercover operative) to provide access and sensitive information.
- Monitoring and exploiting of social media by competitors or government agencies. These media can provide insider information on activities, travel, and provide a means by which employees can be recruited for spying or hired away for their knowledge and information.
- Trash covering (dumpster diving) of businesses and residences to find paper or other sources of information that have been thrown, relatively intact, into the trash.
- Using "honey traps" or "honey pots" (where sex is involved). For example, a female agent seduces a male employee who has access to important information and then uses social engineering to elicit this information. The technique is not limited to male employees being targeted. In one case I dealt with, a female visitor was at a bar near the office and a charming, handsome male got her drunk and stole her company badge, which he used to thwart the access control system and move around the offices at night removing sensitive documents and materials.

It is also important to know if there are companies or countries where the threat levels for business espionage are high and warrant special business and/or travel considerations. Widespread knowledge of the threat—the "who, what, when, where, why and how—is very important to mentally prepare staff for the threats they may face. This is the key to having employees that are ready to protect your sensitive information. They will not do it naturally, on their own. They have to understand the threat and know what their role is in the protection of proprietary information.

Businesses That are Victims of Business Spying

One of the most frequently heard comments or questions I hear centers around the mistaken assumption that if I am not working for or own one of the world's larger companies, if the company I work for or own is not "high tech" or defense related, then there is no need to worry about business espionage.

From the case studies and examples explored in this book it should be clear that the size of the company doesn't matter. It also does not matter what kind of business you are in. If you have competition, you are potentially subject to being a victim of business spying. You do not have to be big, and you do not have to be "high tech" to business spies, although the large, multinational firms and the high tech and defense/aerospace manufacturers are certainly targeted.

Some of the examples we have covered in this book include a small bicycle tour company in Beijing, China that was put out of business when its employees stole its customer and pricing lists and then left and formed their own competing company, and a small, single proprietor hardware store in the U.S. that was put out of business when a large chain sent spies into the company using social engineering and got the store's pricing and profit margin information. I encountered another example of a small software company on a flight to Houston, Texas in mid-2014. The business owner told me the company was experiencing problems retaining clients after some employees left and joined the competition, taking knowledge of their customer base and technical knowledge with them. He acknowledged that the company had not thought much about the threat of business espionage prior to this happening because they did not think they were big enough. While a large automotive or aerospace company will suffer if they lose a million dollars to business-spying efforts, they will probably not go out of business over such a loss. But a loss like this would completely wipe out at least 60 percent of smaller businesses. In my experience the small hardware store and bicycle tour company went out of business as a result of allowing business spies to gather critical information that made their business no longer viable.

While high-tech multinationals and defense-related companies are often targeted many other businesses are small, including a portable toilet manufacturer, a small restaurant chain, a toy designer and maker, a golf-club manufacturer, food producers, hospitals/clinics, law firms, security companies, a bathroom/kitchen fixture manufacturer, a dim sum manufacturer, a paint store, a compressor manufacturer, a small commercial printing firm, an accounting firm, an electronic game maker, a bakery, a publishing firm, a milk company, a soft drink bottling company, and a furniture manufacturer were all actively and successfully targeted by business spies. While none of them thought they needed to be concerned with business espionage, they were all wrong. Other examples included large aerospace companies, computer manufacturers, automobile manufacturers, film companies, software companies, missile manufacturers, and food companies. Given their size and, in some cases, potential military applications of some of their equipment, it is obvious why they may have been targeted.

But the bottom line is that it does not matter how big your company is or what line of business you are in—you can be targeted for business espionage if you have a successful or even marginally successful business. The more successful you are, the more likely you will be targeted but no one is immune.

When I give presentations on business spying I like to ask those in the audience if there is anyone attending who does not have any competition. I ask those without any competition to raise their hand and let me know. In all of hundreds of presentations I have given around the world, only one time has a hand gone up. I asked the individual who raised his hand about his business and found out that he had a company that went around and recovered uniforms or other property from former employees such as hospitals, bus companies, security companies, etc. He said his business was very successful and no one else was doing what he was doing. A year later I saw this same individual at another conference. He came up and told me that one of his employees had taken a lot of his business away by opening a competing company. He said he just wanted to let me know that he now had competition and had suffered losses because of business spying. He added that he should have listened more closely the first time he attended my presentation, but that he just could not believe it would ever happen to him.

Vulnerabilities

We also identified a number of vulnerabilities from the spy case studies and examples given. What is clear is that there are many different methods business spies can employ to steal sensitive business information. Usually business spies use multiple means. They might, for example, get some information from stealing trash and from social engineering. After gaining some pieces of information from these means, they may plant covert electronic spying devices or download computer or other electronically/digitally stored information. They might also distract employees with social engineering and then physically penetrate an office area to steal documents and laptops or get to the company servers.

The threats of business espionage are real and are growing, so it is important for companies to understand this burgeoning threat and to pass on this understanding to employees.

Vulnerability Analysis

What are some of the vulnerabilities we see emerging from the spy incidents and case studies that set the stage for the necessary countermeasures? One of the biggest vulnerabilities I see over and over again is that most companies and most of the staff within these companies are not knowledgeable of the breadth of possible threats and the techniques used by business spies, which has an adverse impact on the company's ability to protect its sensitive information. This boils down to inadequate education and awareness programs that are tailored based on function and access to information.

Another major problem is that almost no companies provide good, up-to-date business-espionage-related travel security information to their travelers. This could be a sub-set of the overall education and awareness problem, but it is especially important because history shows us that this lack of business espionage awareness is a major contributor to the loss of sensitive information.

Another issue that comes up over and over again is the lack of education and awareness training on spotting, reporting, and dealing with social engineering efforts. If staff are trained on the threat and realize that business espionage is not James Bond movie stuff...it is real...they can be alert for social engineering techniques and know to report it and how to thwart it. The training needs differ for secretaries, receptionists, sales and marketing staff, contracting/procurement, and even company leadership, but it is an important aspect of an effective counterespionage program.

The leadership issue is especially important when it comes to what is being protected. There is a sound security principle at stake here that we mentioned in Chapter 7: You cannot protect everything all of the time with limited resources. Since every business entity has limited resources, it is important to determine where the most critical information and resources are located and in what form—those that can have the biggest potential adverse impact on the business. Many company leaders like to say "everything and everybody is important." Perhaps that is true but not everything is equally important. Loss of some things could be more catastrophic for the survival or success of the business than other things, and leaders need to focus on identifying the most important resources that need protected.

Many companies also do not adequately identify and mark all of their sensitive information. As a result, employees do not always understand what is sensitive and what is not. When marking information with appropriate security caveats becomes an important part of a company's culture, there will be a basic understanding. Until that happens there will inevitably be gaps in protection. Additionally, it is worth noting that if information is not properly identified, it loses some of its legal protection in many jurisdictions where there are laws for protecting trade and business secrets. This information must be identified and marked to get the protection warranted.

Of course, most of us know that private businesses operate for profit, which means there must be a return on investment. In order to determine the needed investment in security measures, and in some jurisdictions in order to get protection from laws, it is important to determine the value of all trade secrets and sensitive information you want to protect. In order to do this, a good process for determining the value of intellectual property and sensitive business information is needed.

Given the fact that much of a company's sensitive information is usually stored on IT systems, it is important to focus on protecting IT systems from espionage threats. In my experience IT departments are often better than most entities when it comes to information security. IT is often good about handling external threats but sometimes overlook internal threats. IT can often be weaker, too, when it comes to physical security threats, and the two threats (physical and IT/cyber) are inter-related when it comes to business spying.

Poor access control and a lack of understanding when it comes to the ultimate objective of access control, for example, enables individuals to move around within an area and successfully steal sensitive information. Too many companies look at access control as a system that includes a lot of locks, key cards, and readers. But employees often allow tailgating and I have accessed areas because of naïve employee courtesy and wandered around for hours without anyone ever challenging me. In one case I was invited into an office party even though I was not an employee and was not wearing any identification. One of our penetration specialists got on to the production floor of a food manufacturer, took pictures of the production process, and then, after hours of exploitation, attempted to turn himself into security so the penetration could be recorded. It took him nearly 30 minutes to get anyone from the company or contract security to read the letter he carried and identify him as a penetration tester. One security officer was in such a hurry to check a door alarm that she would not stop and talk with the source of the alarm, which was the very person who was trying to explain this to her. This is another aspect of education and awareness training.

Too often there is no one with expertise on business spying techniques monitoring the CCTV and access control records to try and determine if there are any warning signs related to early detection of possible business espionage. As we have noted, early detection of casing activities or attempts to enter a secure area can be critically important to preventing a business-spying success. Likewise, it is important to know who is coming into work areas and the times they are entering. Once again, unusual work hours that make no business sense can be considered a "red flag." This is an important part of getting full value out of these security systems and using the information to protect your business secrets.

In the same vein, it is important for IT to have monitoring capabilities and to regularly review user activity to see if unusual amounts of information are being downloaded or transferred and to determine if someone might be using another's IT account. This kind of pro-active, preventative IT security could be critical to thwarting a long-term espionage situation. Organizations can implement this type of employee monitoring through a variety of options including the installation of keystroke logging software/hardware and/or packet sniffers on their computer systems/networks. Keystroke logging software/hardware create encrypted log files that store a record of the keystroke or typing activities of a computer user. These flies are stored in a manner invisible to the computer user on either their system's hard drive or other microchips. An example of these monitoring technologies is the Spy Agent software package.[2] This software permits IT or other security staff to monitor the keystroke, instant messaging, and Internet exchange activities of computer users. Packet sniffers perform a similar monitoring function. When placed on a computer network by IT personnel, packet sniffers physically

---

[2] http://www.spy-software-solutions.com

collect system message traffic and data transfers that are initiated by computer users. If IT or security personnel responsible for the monitoring have knowledge of what is sensitive and the specific organizational and individual responsibilities, monitoring of these log files or packet sniffers can often reveal activities by employees as they use organizational computer systems to copy, download, otherwise store, or email trade secrets or other sensitive information. This type of monitoring software could have permitted Avery Dennison to detect Victor Lee's alleged fraudulent use of the computer user names and passwords of fellow employees to access sensitive information from his computer.[3] While Lee's activities might have been detected through these types of monitoring systems, most security specialists would recommend further mitigating this problem by reminding employees, through IT security education and awareness training to (a) change their computer passwords frequently and (b) not to share these passwords with colleagues. These precautions should be communicated to all employees through mandatory security awareness training programs. Any efforts by employees to get co-workers to violate this policy and share passwords should also be reported.

A 2001 survey of employers by the American Management Association revealed that workplace monitoring of employees for security purposes was being conducted by some companies, but is probably not as common as it should be, especially when individuals have access to, and work with, sensitive and protected business information. The survey indicated that (a) 46 percent of responding organizations said they monitored employee email activities, (b) another 36 percent monitored retrieval of computer files by employees, (c) more than 40 percent monitored employee telecommunications, and (d) some 33 percent used CCTV (video surveillance) to enhance security.[4] Some cynics will argue that you cannot monitor employees because of legal protections and restrictions. Yes, there are restrictions but there are ways to deal with the restrictions of laws such as the U.S. Electronic Communications Privacy Act (ECPA), probably the most prominent among them. There are similar laws within the European Union and other countries.

Despite the frequency with which workplace monitoring of employees is conducted by organizations, its use is subject to legal limitations under the ECPA or other similar statutes and

---

[3] Ira Winkler, *Corporate Espionage*, Prima Publishing, 1997.
[4] American Management Association survey: "Workplace Monitoring and Surveillance: Policies and Practices," November 11, 2001, http://www.amanet.org/research/pdfs/emsfu_short.pdf

regulations. The ECPA act addresses the use of wire, oral, or electronic transmission technologies to disseminate information or other communications. It also prohibits the interception and distribution of intercepted communications obtained through the monitoring of these technologies. However, the laws tend to permit certain business exceptions. For example, most laws and regulations note that when employees intentionally misuse organizational telecommunication systems, they are not entitled to any reasonable expectation that their communications will not be subject to monitoring. Misuse of telecommunication systems by employees can include their disclosure of sensitive proprietary information or trade secrets. Additionally, oral or electronic transfer of information can also typically be monitored if employees have both given their consent to and been notified of this type of workplace surveillance In the absence of expressed consent, an employer may monitor communications to determine if the communications are of a business or personal nature. Policies and procedures, and education and awareness training, can further qualify that employees were notified and understood the process and reasons. Upon identifying the communication as personal, the law requires that monitoring must be terminated. However, that is a concern from a security perspective because it is possible that employees may engage in a subterfuge to thwart monitoring by initiating communications on a personal basis to circumvent the monitoring. "Clever" employees would then presume they were free to communicate proprietary information without fear of detection. Therefore, in addition to obtaining express consent to monitor workplace activities, companies should also (1) establish and enforce prohibitions against the personal and non-business use of organizational computer and telecommunications systems, (2) post written and electronic notification of these prohibitions and make it clear that it is the policy of the company to monitor all employee communications, and (3) create a business rationale for employee monitoring and implement this security program/approach in an equitable manner. One of the ways to do this is to link this monitoring program with the functions of those who have access to the company's protected and sensitive business information.[5]

There are some restrictions that require legal oversight before implementation, but companies can and do monitor communications and doing this can provide a deterrent and allow for early detection of possible inappropriate handling of, or transfer of,

[5] Electronic Communications Privacy Act, 1986: 18 U.S. Code, Section 2511, 2701.

sensitive proprietary information. Human Resources (HR) often does not know and understand the various threats posed by business espionage and are unable to appropriately screen prospective employees or current employees for indicators of possible business spying or vulnerability to recruitment. Financial problems, drug issues, attendance issues, and foreign ties all can be linked to business espionage and my experience is that almost no one in HR ever thinks of that possible linkage and reports it so it can be looked at again. One spy was living way beyond his means. He owned multiple sports cars and didn't even quickly cash his checks issued for expenses. After it was reported that he was a spy, all of his co-workers and even some members of the HR staff said they were not surprised and thought back about strange things he had done. Finance knew he had not cashed all of his checks, but no one reported this to security. The damage was already done. With well-trained staff, a reporting method, and a review mechanism these situations would have resulted in an early investigation that could then have prevented many of the losses. The lack of an anonymous reporting method for business espionage and the failure to encourage employees to use the reporting process can be a major vulnerability. Unfortunately, it is a frequently missing element in many business counterespionage programs.

Contractors such as cleaning staff, security, and other functions contracted out are too often given unescorted access to sensitive areas such as research and development laboratories, executive offices, and server areas. Many companies do not have designed high-security areas where individuals, especially contractors, are not allowed by themselves (a "no lone zone").

One of the bigger vulnerabilities, but one that is often overlooked, is just plain carelessness and accidental disclosures/losses. These often occur without any bad intentions but the result can be the same as an overt espionage act in terms of the adverse impact on the company. If an adversary is watching and waiting, even a careless disclosure, such as an accidental discard of a sensitive document in the trash can result in a loss. Having an entity (perhaps security) that regularly checks for accidental disclosures by doing things like trash checks can be a valuable way to identify vulnerabilities and then handling them.

It is important to have good security-related policies and procedures designed specifically to protect sensitive information from business espionage threats. Many companies have security-related policies and procedures but few of those specifically address business espionage. The objective of such policies and procedures, among other things, is to ensure education and awareness, establish protection parameters, and ensure reporting, investigation, and tracking of any possible business-spying attempts. These areas are rarely addressed in the security policies and procedures I have reviewed. Yet they can easily fit in education and awareness programs. They can also establish that the company has taken specific measures to protect its secrets and prove to be deterrents for would-be spies.

All employees and contractors should be required to (but often are not) to sign non-disclosure, non-compete, and other legal documents designed to protect specifically protected information. No one should share any of this information with anyone until he or she is absolutely certain (assuming is not acceptable) such agreements have been legally executed for the jurisdiction(s) involved. Once again, this rarely is done because people are often more concerned about getting things done than protecting what they are doing. The key is to do both.

Many times there also are inadequate procedures and capabilities to protect sensitive documents and electronic information that is being placed for sale or destruction. A number of companies use shredders or pulverizers but these are usually centrally located, and employees, who are generally creatures of convenience, use them only if it is convenient. The result is sensitive documents are stored in unlocked containers or piles under desks or they are torn up (if employees do anything) and thrown into the regular trash. Some companies have centralized, locked destruction bins and use a destruction service, but the key here is to have the destruction monitored, which is usually not done. I have actually done surveillances of destruction companies where destruction company employees were in the back of a truck looking through documents and the company was totally unaware of it. Destruction of electromagnetic devices and old computer, old copiers/printers, etc., is also important. The storage drives of these devices must also be cleaned or destroyed.

Similarly, too many companies do not have a "clean desk" policy. It never ceases to amaze me when I walk through offices and cubicles in businesses around the world that there are so many areas where documents and other materials are left stacked high and unsecured. Computers or portable hard drives are also often left unsecured. Companies should require all sensitive documents and materials be secured in locked rooms, cabinets, or safes when not in use and regular checks should be made to ensure compliance.

Facility staff and event planners are also too often oblivious to the threats posed by business espionage when selecting office or event sites. It is important to know who owns the building, hotel, or what other businesses (as in competitors) that might be sharing a multi-tenant building where you are locating your operations. If you are holding an event where sensitive information could be discussed such as a regional operations meeting, a sales or marketing planning meeting, or a board of directors meeting, make sure security is a part of decisions on locations, etc. Given the ease at which electronic eavesdropping can occur in the twenty-first century, secure areas, offices, conference rooms, and event rooms should receive a thorough pro-active TSCM sweep, especially in high-threat environments. Once again, this almost never occurs, and if it does, it is all too often after-the-fact and reactive.

Companies that believe they have outstanding security for protecting their sensitive information from business spies should consider penetration testing to ensure they are correct in their assessment of their security effectiveness. Conducting physical and IT/cyber tests of security can ensure that counter-espionage measures are effective or, if there is an issue, the vulnerability uncovered during the test can be identified and the gap closed.

It is important to conduct a vulnerability assessment (as a part of a holistic risk assessment) that looks for these kinds of vulner-abilities. While some are "traditional" physical or IT/cyber secu-rity issues some are not, and even traditional issues often have unique aspects that need to be considered. Regardless, knowing the typical vulnerabilities to spying that are faced in the business world can be an important aspect of establishing appropriate security standards and ensuring they are met.

Consequences/Business Impact Analysis

The best way to implement the recommended countermea-sures is to concentrate the majority of security measures on those locations, personnel/functions, and travel that involves sensitive information. Many of the recommended countermeasures can help with deterring, detecting, and neutralizing a variety of crim-inal activities beyond business spying, but by countering business spying a business entity is not throwing expensive and overly restrictive security measures on every aspect of the business. It is, instead, focusing and deploying appropriate measures where they are most needed to protect a company's most sensitive busi-ness information. This is what happens when a company carefully assesses and studies its business processes, information, and determines what is truly sensitive and warrants protection. The focus is on potential adverse business impacts or consequences.

Summary

While the threat of business espionage is widespread and growing, companies do not have to wait to be a victim. There are some core countermeasures that can protect sensitive information, many of which I've shared here. If I had to prioritize them I would say it is vital for any company to know its business secrets and their economic value. It is also important for all employees—but some more than others—to have detailed knowledge of the threats faced and know what to do to protect the company's sensitive information from business spying. Finally, it is important to have good policies, procedures, and standards in place that are based on the potential adverse business impact a loss could bring and that are supported by senior management.

If companies take this risk-based approach to dealing with business espionage, it is possible to protect sensitive business information, and it could mean the difference between business success or failure.

Good luck!

INDEX

Note: Page numbers followed by *f* indicate figures.